French's Cavalry Campaign

General French

French's Cavalry Campaign

A special correspondent's view of
British Army Mounted troops
during the Boer War

J. G. Maydon

LEONAUR

French's Cavalry Campaign
A special corresponent's view of
British Army Mounted troops
during the Boer War
by J. G. Maydon

First published under the titles
French's Cavalry Campaign

Leonaur is an imprint
of Oakpast Ltd

ISBN: 978-1-84677-752-3 (hardcover)
ISBN: 978-1-84677-751-6 (softcover)

http://www.leonaur.com

Publisher's Notes

In the interests of authenticity, the spellings, grammar and place names
used have been retained from the original editions.

The opinions of the authors represent a view of events in which he
was a participant related from his own perspective,
as such the text is relevant as an historical document.

The views expressed in this book are not necessarily
those of the publisher.

Contents

To

The Memory of

David, 8th Earl of Airlie

Who, having devoted his life to his Queen

and to the Service,

paid it out to the uttermost

at Diamond Hill,

after the capture of Pretoria,

falling in the moment of Victory,

and at the head of his Regiment

Preface

This little contribution to the story of the Great War (Boer War) is directed to one end only. It seeks to make plain the part played by an arm, which has come to be considered in some quarters as of but secondary account in war.

A more able writer, with such experience and knowledge as it was my good fortune to acquire, would be able to show conclusively from the events here related that not only is cavalry wholly indispensable in every field of operation—singularly enough it was retained even within the lines of Ladysmith—but that in the successes of this great contest it has played the leading role.

But for misrepresentations on this score I would not have ventured to intrude my version on an already satiated circle of readers, but a witness is necessary, and the unique experience I enjoyed of seeing practically the whole of the cavalry operations, and thereby the solution of the great war problem, calls me to tender my story.

These pages will reveal that round Colesberg was developed that method which in the end was to turn the tide of battle; that round Colesberg was made, a reputation that has not ceased to be one of terror and dismay to the opposing Boer forces; and that the forging of a weapon—the Cavalry Division—was there completed, which was to prove the means not only of laying open the road into Kimberley and into Bloemfontein, but even of effecting the change of circumstance which enabled the long delayed relief of Ladysmith.

Seeing, as I have seen, the operations on the western frontier as far as Bloemfontein, I cannot hesitate to state that, gallant as was the fighting spirit of our infantry, indomitable as was its marching mood, and cheerful as was its endurance, yet it was doomed to a continuance of failure, such as had befallen it at every point during the first four months of the war, unless a means was found, such as was in fact forthcoming, of counteracting the advantages possessed by the Boers, who could lie behind impregnable places so long as they were impregnable, and then move four miles to a new fastness, whilst their pursuers were wearily following after them.

The cavalry arm was the new factor which altered the terms of the equation, as this little story endeavours to set forth.

One word more. Many writers challenge the Cavalry on the ground that the Mounted Infantry will supersede it. My eyes have seen that what the latter can do, the former can do better. The cavalry rides better, nurses its horses more, understands their needs better, and has a generally higher value than the infantryman on horseback. And, making allowance for the difference of arm, shoots not less well.

But by all means perfect the Mounted Infantryman. Only let him be what his name assumes. Use him as an infantryman on horseback, to be moved quickly and with little fatigue to any salient point.

Don't make the mistake of thinking him of equal value for patrol or *vidette* work, or imagine him the very thing in a pursuit.

On the other hand, let us frankly recognise that we must make many and great improvements in our cavalry.

We must provide a better carbine, or a rifle instead of a carbine.

We must find means of carrying food for men and horses along with the men, but not on their horses.

We must contrive to lighten all saddlery and accoutrements without impairing strength or efficiency.

And finally, we must silence those hasty critics who roundly assert that sword and lance must go into the limbo of the past. One or the other, with the conditions of the last paragraph applied, must still be carried. And not until morale ceases to be an ingredient in making an army must we permit ourselves to listen to the unconsidered advice which bids us sweep such weapons into the museums.

The lance especially held for the Boer a greater terror than all our artillery put together.

Our horse gunners were worthy of the cavalry they accompanied, and surely worthy of a more effective weapon than they possessed; nevertheless, with a gun unceasingly outranged, they proved continually capable not only of silencing the opposing gun, but of the far more arduous task of subduing rifle-fire while well within its range.

Never in the history of the nation has it owed so much to the unostentatious service of its horse-soldiers, and never have those soldiers proved abler for stupendous effort.

Let us try, then, to *render unto Caesar the things that are Caesar's*, and even to a cavalryman his due.

In acknowledging the kind permission to dedicate these pages to the memory of the gallant Earl of Airlie, I wish to say that my views have no claim to be considered as expressions of his opinion.

Jno. G. Maydon.

Introduction

That a struggle between the two Caucasian races in South Africa was so impossible an occurrence as the surface politician and the general mass of the inhabitants of Great Britain believed, nobody would maintain who had either lived observantly in the Transvaal for the ten years, or in the Orange Free State for the five years, before the war, or who had studied the story of the two peoples, particularly in relation to the Cape.

It may be judicious, before dealing with that portion of the late war upon which the issue of the contest turned, to devote a few pages to a brief review of the relations between these races from the early days of the settlement onwards, in order that we may better follow the nature of the struggle in which we have lately been engaged.

That any echoes of the sea-fights of De Ruyter and Van Tromp and his successors should reach the ears of their descendants two centuries later may seem incredible, yet it is but a particular instance of the general principle of patriotism, which proved in our own case so active that the call to arms echoed from the snows of Canada to the plains of Australia, and from the fenced fields of England to the wild forests of Burmah; and indeed the spirit of the quarrel which deposed Holland from the command of the seas has descended to the untutored and rough children of the old sea heroes.

If there are many worthy things they have forgotten, they have at least remembered that a Dutch fleet passed the greatest humiliation on England she has ever sustained, and have been willing to try and repeat in these days on land the triumphs of their forefathers. Nor is it so wonderful after all that these memories of two centuries ago should be so permanent when we consider that the forefathers of the Boer of today came straight to Africa from those very contests, and that the feeling of national rivalry was kept alive by the struggle for supremacy between the Dutch East India Company and the English East India Company, the fight being made real to the people in the Cape by reason of the settlement there being a most important arsenal for the Dutch Company, which was indeed the means of establishing the first Dutch colonists in Africa.

For a century the Dutch at the Cape took some part in this protracted fight; they were held under a form of military service by the Governors of the Dutch Company ruling at Cape Town, and they speedily came to hate the Dutch Company and its ways as cordially as they have ever since detested all forms of control. Thus the Cape settlement became a kind of shuttlecock tossed to and fro between the two nations, coming twice under British control, and passing back to the Dutch before it was finally handed over to England by the Treaty of Paris in return for a very substantial subsidy to Holland.

England first occupied it at the request of the *Stadtholder*, to prevent the French seizing so important a post; and the occupation was made not a day too soon, a fact of some interest when one so often hears the charge levelled against our own country by our own countrymen of greedy oppression shown towards the Dutch in Africa.

Early in the present century, then, English rule was established at Cape Town, and England assumed the governance of a people who started with hereditary tendencies of enmity towards her, strengthened by a contest (of which they had been the witnesses and in part the object) between the Dutch colonial system and the English, and who, having conceived against the control of the Dutch Company a detestation so pronounced that it had led to overt acts of rebellion, found themselves transferred with all these independent sentiments to a people they hated nationally.

One must admit that the new colony began therefore under ill auspices, and a very light hand and very judicious driving were needed to prevent the team from capsizing the coach. But unfortunately in the early years of the century judicious treatment of colonists was the last thing to be expected of the English Government; the methods which had driven America to fight the Mother Country still prevailed, and there were two questions involved in the position in South Africa which were destined to produce endless trouble.

The first of these was the native, who was perennially at war with the Dutch farmers on the outskirts of the slowly expanding settlement. Into the merits of these quarrels it is needless to inquire, but the cancellation of the terms of a treaty, arranged by the Dutch leaders with the native chiefs and having the approval of the British Governor at Cape Town, marked the culminating point of discontent, and led to the Great Trek of 1837—the occupation of the Orange Free State, and the crossing of the Drakensberg into Natal, the coast of which was already in English hands.

The second was the liberation of the slaves. The entire servant class amongst the Dutch settlers was servile, necessarily servile, for the Bantu and Hottentot races perform all work through their women, the occupations of the men being war and hunting. Even such manual labour as breaking up the soil or hewing wood is done by women, consequently the Dutch settlers could not carry on their farming operations except by coercion. Suddenly, by the philanthropic sentiment of a people entirely ignorant of the heavy conditions under which life was born in South Africa, the Dutch were deprived of their servants and farm hands; for "liberation" meant, almost universally, the withdrawal of the labouring class, the inducement of pay being quite an insufficient substitute for coercion. Nor was this all; the sum of money provided as compensation by England for the owners of slaves set free by the will of the English people was subject to all kinds of malversation, and reached the claimants, where it reached them at all, a greatly attenuated stream.

But with all this series of misunderstandings and ineptitudes, the sum of our blundering was by no means reached, for arising out of "the Great Trek," and the acquirement of fresh territory, came the necessity for assuming some control over the lawlessness which everywhere sprang up amongst a people who, whilst expanding their territorial possessions by force, made no attempt to establish any form of law and order under which to live at peace. Thus in Natal actual war broke out when English Courts, undertaking the settlement of the country, allocated certain land reservations to the natives.

In the Orange River Colony a British Resident had been established by the request of the Dutch, the country was proclaimed in 1845 British territory, a small garrison was stationed at Bloemfontein, and magistrates were appointed to maintain order. But one, Andries Pretorius, being delegated to represent certain grievances as to land grants, which had indeed no real foundation other than greed, was rudely refused an audience by Sir H. Pottinger, the English Governor, and retired to raise a revolt in the sovereignty; this was only put down by Sir Harry Smith, Pottinger's successor, who attacked the Boer forces at Boomplaats, completely scattering the rebels, and reinstating the British Resident.

But after six years England grew weary of the burden, and in 1854, despite the protests not only of English residents, but also of the most prosperous of the Dutch, the English flag was hauled down, and a Republic established, and though this Republic has had up to the present day a most prosperous career, and at times useful assistance from England, yet it nurses an old resentment, inasmuch as England assumed sovereignty over what it regarded as part of its territory (*viz.*, Griqualand West) as soon as the discovery of diamonds was followed by an influx of foreign population, or, as the Dutch regard it, as soon as the country had become valuable.

The history of the Transvaal presents a curiously close parallel to that of the Orange Free State. The country, first settled by Boers, came to financial straits in the effort to maintain an orderly form of government, and invited English intervention, which was granted in accordance with the will of the Dutch inhabitants, as is pretty conclusively demonstrated by the fact that Sir (or as he then was, Mr.) Theophilus Shepstone's escort was practically without ammunition when it accompanied him to Pretoria to proclaim the Transvaal English territory; and discontent speedily arose on the part of the less prosperous of the Dutch inhabitants, eventuating in the war of 1881.

Such, briefly, has been the political history of this people, and its conspicuous characteristic is an original hostility perpetually irritated and renewed.

The mode of life pursued by the Dutch people is admirably fitted to produce men capable of engaging in, and long maintaining, a war against even powerful odds. Until quite recently, the rifle stood with the Boer in the stead of the plough to the European agriculturist, for not only was it necessary for safety, but the food the settler ate and the clothes he wore were alike provided by its means, and all the necessaries of life were obtained by exchange for the skins it gathered.

Not only was a very great proficiency in the handling of arms thus attained, but that wonderful knowledge of country which has been equal to a spare horse for every man in this campaign, that woodcraft (or *veldtcraft* perhaps one had better say) was acquired, whose principles are those—on a less extended scale perhaps, but still the same—which control the movements of armies, and that habit of open-air life, which has enabled an entire people to take the field, and for so long to maintain a campaign without anything approaching the expenses or the cumbersomeness which are unavoidable in a more regular force, and which would have quickly brought the present struggle to an end. Boer successes have been achieved only because of this radical difference of method between themselves and the English.

Each man also was actuated by a strong contempt for his foe, in part due to the easy victory achieved in 1881; in part to the hasty concession of freedom, for though the English Premier had forensically declared it unjust to withhold it, he had nevertheless entered upon war rather than surrender it; and in part to the general character of that portion of the English race which mainly came under Boer observation, and which certainly was not of a kind to impress him with any belief in the qualities which have made the nation what it is.

Thus, then, the Dutch patriot had conceived the notion of stepping into an Empire readymade, which was dropping from the feeble hands of a race emasculated by wealth and an unchallenged possession of the earth. Events had conspired to give form to his dream, for quickly following his acquisition of self-government in the Transvaal, the discovery of gold had put such power of wealth into his hands that the means of arming with the most formidable weapons science has as yet evolved were at his command, and the means also of purchasing such support from the Continental enemies of England, as appeared to his too credulous mind equal to at least an army corps; and all this led him to expect a certainty of intervention should he indeed be worsted.

Nor should one, in estimating the forces at work to animate the Boer mind, omit to reckon his extraordinarily active and real belief in the interposition of the Almighty. Such of the Western Nations as hold to the belief that God indeed shapes the destinies of nations and the issues of war, regard His power as manifesting itself through the wisdom of the rulers preparing for war, and the skill of the warriors fighting the battle, both vouchsafed to the victorious nation by His will, but the Dutch believed in His personal intervention as materially as in the days of Jericho. They have that curious obsession of mind which enables them to regard themselves as worthy of everything good and their enemies as wholly the reverse; so curious because, though the standard of English morality is perhaps lower in South Africa than in most places equally English in character, it is still in every single respect so vastly higher than the Dutch, that comparison becomes ridiculous.

Perhaps this conviction is even then not so surprising as is the coincident belief that prevails (ought I to say "prevailed") at home, that the Boer is compounded of the highest virtues. Instead of that, he is mean, dirty, immoral, dishonest, so untruthful that he will lie even though he is aware that his hearer knows the truth and will not be deceived, so unashamed that he would rather be thought a "slim Karel" than a Bayard, and so impervious to disgrace that it was a weekly occurrence to read in a Dutch paper an apology from one Boer to another, in which the offender characterised himself with every base and opprobrious epithet in tendering his public apology.

Yet in face of all this, and while it is hard to understand how self-deception could go to the length of believing that the Almighty would prefer the low and dirty wickedness of the Boer to the robuster sins of the English, the Boer warriors were actually inspired to expect that they would be upheld by the God of Righteousness, Who would wholly turn His face from their English adversaries.

Herein, then, one sees the foreshadowing of those events which form the subject of my narrative, and from these facts one can better trace back the logical sequence of effect to cause.

CHAPTER 1

Preparing an Advance

When, towards the close of 1899, General Sir Redvers Buller landed at Cape Town to take up his command, practically the only forces we had in South Africa were beleaguered by the Boers, and, but for two batteries which had already arrived, there were no signs as yet of the expected Army Corps. The situation was by no means cheerful, and before many hours elapsed the outlook was gloomier still, for news reached Cape Town of the fiasco at Nicholson's Nek, and the loss of a mountain battery with about 1100 men of the Gloucesters and the Royal Irish.

The magnitude of the struggle England had entered upon only now began to manifest itself even to the minds of the generally well informed. Many important English daily papers, for instance, either had no representatives in the country, or had so few as to be unable to keep in touch with the very widely spread operations, and it was at this time that I received an invitation to act as correspondent for the *Daily News* in the Cape Colony.

I had come from England with a desire to play a more belligerent role in Natal, the land of my adoption, and somewhat protracted residence, and to Natal I proceeded. Arrived there, however, I found that there was rather a disinclination to accept the service of volunteers than an eagerness to receive them, while the urgency of my friend the agent for the *Daily News* impressed on me the wider usefulness which I might render the colony through the press than I could hope to do by trailing a musket; this, added to the unwillingness one feels to press a service one discovers is not greatly desired, led me to retrace my steps to the Cape Colony.

General French, having dashed up to Ladysmith the day he landed from England, had arrived just in time to be entrusted by Sir G. White with the operations necessary to clear the retreat of Penn Symons' victorious but outnumbered troops from Talana. The Boers had intercepted the line of retreat, and were sitting astride the railway at Elandslaagte, sixteen miles north of Ladysmith and thirty-five miles south of Dundee. French, with a small compact force, fell upon them late in the day on October 20, and inflicted a severe defeat, practically destroying the foreign contingent recruited in Johannesburg, and enabling Symons' force, now under Yule, to retire unmolested to Ladysmith. This brilliant little action was fought by infantry, for in it the Imperial Light Horse fought as such, and commenced a roll of achievements which may well be the generous envy of any regiment or corps.

Having opened a road for Yule and Dartnell (and to the last-named the country owes a stupendous debt of gratitude, for in no small degree the successful achievement of the retreat was due to him), it seems to have occurred to French that it would be well, while there was yet time, to return to headquarters; thus, by the last train that got away, the man round whom for many months to come the only gleam of success of all the campaign was to shine, escaped from Ladysmith.

Why, since it was clear to so many minds that a siege was inevitable, the opportunity had not been taken of sending down the cavalry, whose usefulness outside was infinitely more than within the defended circle, has not yet been explained. It will be interesting to have this point made clear.

General French, at any rate, had got out with his staff, and promptly returned to the western theatre of the war, being sent to Nauwport, a junction on the Midland system of the Cape railways, where an important depot had been in course of formation.

Maitland Camp: Regimental Mule Transport

General Buller had by this time found the full measure of the task that lay before him, and signalised his opening of the campaign by a disastrous and costly mistake. Admittedly he had an utter insufficiency of troops for the fearfully extended lines of communication, to say nothing of maintaining an offensive force at either extremity of those lines; nevertheless the order to abandon the Stormberg and Nauwport was most disastrous, and at once brought about the invasion of that part of the Cape frontier for which the disloyal inhabitants had long been asking. Happily, before the evacuation of Nauwport was complete, the order was countermanded, stores which had been removed were returned, General French was nominated to the command there, and a cavalry brigade was to be collected under him.

Had the original intention been carried out, the only line of communication which would have remained in our hands would have been that between Cape Town and Orange River *via* De Aar; all the Midland districts of the Cape Colony down to Graaf Reinet and Cradock would have been "up," and the main line must almost certainly have fallen also.

The Stormberg was immediately occupied by the Boers under Olivier, and our troops' most advanced post, on the East London line, was at Molteno and Sterkstroom, only eleven miles farther back, but now fronting a formidable position held by the Boers instead of holding it against them.

Gatacre was to pay the penalty of all this that black week in December.

Having left Natal on November 19, 1899, in order to witness Lord Methuen's effort to relieve Kimberley, on which all the strength of the western campaign was directed, there was some doubt whether I should be up in time. Men who had an excellent knowledge of the Dutch people, their preparations and determination, still would not believe that they could successfully withstand Lord Methuen's force.

Reaching De Aar about midnight, November 23, I found farther progress barred until the arrival of a press permit from Cape Town, and only after invoking the kind aid of Colonel

Troops for the Front

Hanbury Williams by telegraph from Cape Town, did I escape being ignominiously bundled back, but neither this nor a direct wire from the censor at Cape Town sufficed to enable me to get forward.

During the day the first battle had been fought and won. The Boers, holding a strong position at Belmont, twenty-one miles beyond the Orange River, and ninety from De Aar, had been attacked by Lord Methuen, and after a stubborn resistance the hills commanding the railway were captured, the Guards Brigade suffering heavily. Some prisoners were taken, and some wagons, stores, and ammunition fell into our hands, or were burnt, but the Boers got off without any of the serious consequences of defeat, Methuen being deficient in cavalry and guns.

The 9th Lancers were indeed his only cavalry; he had also Major Rimington's corps of guides, but these together did not supply a sufficiency of men for the enormously heavy patrol work necessary in such a country, and against an enemy every man of whom was mounted. Neither at Belmont, therefore, nor Graspan was there any cavalry for pursuit, the enemy retiring and getting off his guns in the most leisurely manner. To this impunity the subsequent course of events is largely traceable.

Retiring to Graspan, only eight miles distant, Delarey took ground in a very strong position again astride the railway, where two days later he was again attacked, and the day was won with comparatively slight loss; but unfortunately a portion of the position which had already become untenable was stormed by the Naval Brigade, who carried the *kopje* most gallantly, but with heavy loss.

This was an absolutely fruitless victory. Behind the Boer position a beautiful flat country lay, across which they had to retire, and our batteries missed an opportunity of which, too, they had been made aware, and the gallant 9th tried in vain to raise a gallop from horses which had been continuously under the saddle for thirty hours.

The same day that brought news of this barren victory brought also news that the Boers had occupied Stormberg in

Boers Wounded at Belmont

strength.

Despairing now of ever getting the necessary papers, and thinking events might move quickly against Olivier, I was permitted to proceed to Nauwport, which was now cut off from the port of East London, and from any direct communication with Gatacre's division operating from thence.

French had a somewhat mixed force under him at Nauwport, and circumstances made it difficult to collect even a brigade; but with the 12th Lancers and less than 200 Australian and New South Wales lancers, supported at headquarters by a splendid battalion of the old 66th (the Berkshires) and by the Black Watch, he was already covering a very wide front and pressing back Commandant Schoeman, whose men had actually blown up a small bridge within a mile of the station on the line to De Aar, though happily not very effectively, for the traffic was never really interrupted.

Nor did French give them time ever again to undertake offensive operations in this locality; strong patrols and reconnaissances pushed daily farther and farther north; disloyal residents were arrested under the very noses of the Boer commando and brought to jail, and the country was cleared as far as Arundel, twenty-one miles north, a position of great natural strength. At this stage I made the acquaintance of the officers of the 12th Lancers, a regiment whom its gallant colonel, Lord Airlie, had brought to a very high state of efficiency, and it was my good fortune to be with them for more than a month without intermission, and to see with them some very splendid service.

CHAPTER 2

Methuen and Modder River

On arriving at Nauwport I had presented myself at headquarters, and from Major Haig and Captain Lawrence found that, though there was plenty to do and see every day, the impossibility of collecting a force adequate to undertake a movement of real importance rendered it undesirable to remain there and miss the more stirring events of the main line of advance.

Accordingly, when the 12th Lancers were ordered up to join Lord Methuen, who had meantime sustained practically a repulse at the Modder River, I obtained permission to accompany them, resolving that at the earliest opportunity I would come back to observe the conduct of any operations that might fall to the lot of the indefatigable little Irish cavalryman (General French). I saw too, or thought I saw, in Major (now Colonel) Haig a chief of staff of no small ability, and of a singular grasp of the special qualities needful to solve the problem of subduing the wily Boer, whilst I then thought, as I still think, Captain (now Major) Lawrence the best intelligence officer of the campaign.

On December 2, therefore, bidding a temporary farewell to General French and his staff, I found myself at last *en route* for the Kimberley relief force with the 12th Lancers, and the next evening we detrained about four miles short of Modder River, the line to the rail head being blocked with rolling-stock. A ramp of sleepers enabled this admirable regiment to detrain rapidly, and it had taken up its ground on the north bank of the

Modder before midnight, though it was as dark as pitch.

The air was foul with the decaying carcasses of animals killed in the battle of the preceding Tuesday (November 28), and the burying parties had not even then finished their dismal task. Lord Methuen's Division was exhausted, not to say discouraged, by the severe shaking it had sustained in wresting the passage of the river from the enemy.

Three heavy engagements had already been fought, and in each the troops, after heroic behaviour, had won a barren victory, inflicting far less severe loss than they sustained.

The two previous battles at Belmont and Graspan might well have been expected to disclose to Lord Methuen the nature of the task before him. They had indeed disclosed the facility with which the Boer drew off when he could no longer withstand the attack; how easily he got away his guns and ammunition and the bulk of his stores and munitions.

They might also have been expected to demonstrate that the enemy in front of him had an unequalled facility for taking rapid advantage of the lie of the ground, and a splendid obstinacy in contesting every inch of it, so long at least as the line of retreat was not threatened; and every hunter in the country knew and would have told Lord Methuen—doubtless all with whom he talked did tell him—that this was the weak joint in the Boer armour. Be that as it may, it was abundantly clear that the cavalry arm Methuen had with him was lamentably weak for scouting and outpost work, and entirely inadequate for flanking or pursuit.

It was also clear that the guns were equally inadequate; omitting all count of their value relative to the Boer guns, they had proved wholly unable at Graspan to take any part after the battle was over in cutting up the flying enemy; horses, fagged out with the evolutions of the actual battle, couldn't dash off to harass the retreat. Yet, though there was a sufficiency both of cavalry and guns, not only in the country, but within easy call, no step was taken prior to Modder River to strengthen these arms. Indeed, on the morning of the fight our troops were advancing with

Horses going up to the Front

an amazing and misplaced confidence that there would be no further fighting till Spytfontein.

And yet to have awaited such support would have involved no dangerous delay. Kimberley, the immediate objective, had been cut off for six weeks, its resources were not even beginning to be strained, the fact of a large force advancing to its relief tended to diminish the risks of an assault, for if none had been delivered in the first days of the siege when the whole Boer army was available, and there was no need to detach any portion to check a relieving force, it was not to be expected when such a force was within twenty-five miles of the town.

There was no urgency then in this direction.

That there was none, on the ground that the Boers held a strong natural position which time would enable them to make impregnable, is obvious from the fact that Methuen refused to believe the information given him by the 9th Lancers, that they were entrenching the river banks, and rejected it in favour of local information twenty-four hours older, correct when it was obtained, but incorrect when the advance was made.

We are thus driven back to the theory that the only reason for haste was Methuen's fear that the Boers would evacuate their positions without giving battle.

This should rather have been a motive for delay, because though each of the three battle-grounds afforded a splendid opportunity for cutting up the retiring enemy when driven out of position if strong cavalry and artillery had been to hand, without those arms the enemy must inevitably escape.

On Tuesday morning then, November 28, the division was advancing on a front of about half a mile, with a full belief in the peaceful occupation of the village which lies (a scattered hamlet) on both banks of the river, grown into a respectable stream by the junction of the Riet a few hundred yards above the railway bridge. The bushless Karoo plain slopes down towards the river at a gentle grade for about 2000 yards, ending in a broken sandy bank at various levels, somewhat thickly bushed with mimosa and willows.

THE DRIFT OVER THE MODDER RIVER

A few hours with the spade on the previous day had opened trenches on both banks, those on the south being in three lines, and the rearmost trench continuous for a mile and a quarter.

Our advance was unchallenged until the leading brigade was well under the Boer rifles, when a murderous fire opened, and nailed the living as well as the killed and wounded prone to the earth, where they lay for the rest of the day. In cover no higher than clover, and not so thick, these unhappy troops lay the whole day in a burning sun, and so exposed that even if a water bottle were full it could not be used, for even so slight a movement attracted the deadly Boer bullets.

No more striking commentary can be passed on the day's tactics than that all the wounded Highlanders seemed to be suffering in the legs, and on inquiring the nature of the wounds an enormous percentage was disclosed to be sunburnt between the stockings and the kilt. So exposed was the position, that the men had to lie all day and have the skin burnt off their knees rather than venture to stir enough to screen them.

Half our force was thus out of action, and that was by no means the worst of the situation, for because of it our efforts of the day were more directed to endeavouring to force the immediate front and cover these prostrate battalions than to dealing with the position on its merits, so that it was only late in the day that Brigadier-General Pole-Carew, having been informed that the Yorkshires had thrown a picket into the thorn scrub of the river banks on the extreme left of our attack, and covered what appeared a practicable drift, gathered some units together of the Guards, the Highlanders, and the Yorkshires, and crossed the river.

Clearing the scrubby banks, he advanced to turn the right of the Boer position, which would have been successfully stormed but for the disastrous chance that our own guns opened on his attack as his men crossed the open ground to the west of the railway station and on the north bank of the river, no information having been sent back to them that a passage had been effected. The force, not numerically strong and not homogeneous, could not face the heavy Boer rifle fire, backed by the tremendous shell fire from our own guns, and contented itself with holding the wooded north bank and a neighbouring cottage which it had seized.

The enemy was, however, had we but known it, already in full retreat, believing the day lost. Even the guns were abandoned, and had only a fresh battalion been thrown across the river the whole position would have been taken without further opposition, and the heavy Boer guns would have been captured, standing as they were in the emplacements, whence they had been fought during the day, without an effort having been made at this time to withdraw them.

It was considerably past midnight that some Boers were persuaded to come back and recover these guns, having received information from their friends in the village that the British had not seized them, but were lying exhausted on the ground they had won. It was nearly daylight when the last of these guns was got away, and there was not a soul among the British residents to carry word to our forces of the prize lying unguarded under our hands.

For the third time we had forced the Boer position by sheer dogged fighting, had had the prizes of battle within our grasp, and had missed them partly from ignorance of the fact, and partly for want of means to seize them.

If Inkerman was a soldier's battle, assuredly these three stubborn fights of Belmont, Graspan, and Modder River were not less so, distinguished for the same want of skill in handling our troops, the same ignorance of what the enemy intended, what was his strength, and how to deal with him in the hour of victory.

CHAPTER 3

The Call for Cavalry

Only then did the absolute need for more guns and more cavalry force itself upon the consideration of the commander, and from De Aar and Nauwport, not 200 miles distant by rail, a cavalry regiment (the 12th Lancers) and two batteries were now brought up, whose presence at any one of these three battles would have probably secured Methuen a handsome and substantial triumph, or at any rate have enabled him to harass the Boer retreat, and even have secured the easy relief of Kimberley; for subsequent events were to prove that the magnificent defensive fighting qualities of the Boers crumbled away on the instant their line of retreat was imperilled.

Modder River cost us 485 men killed and wounded, and left us still ten miles short of Spytfontein, which was the main defensive position against our relieving force.

But what was of far more consequence, it affected the fine temper of the steel. The division had behaved magnificently, but the sword had lost its edge. It had been submitted to too fierce a heat. There was a feeling in the air that the relieving force was being used only as a sort of battering-ram, and even when it had been successfully used there was the lack of management to seize the opportunity created thereby.

An army is a very sensitively balanced machine. It will take any sort of treatment from a man it believes in—suffer hunger and want, endure decimation, march the boots off its feet, and all as cheerfully as it would enjoy the best-arranged picnic—but it must feel that the man who asks all this of it has a purpose in the asking, knows not only how to beat his enemy, but how to crumple him up when he is beaten. Given this confidence, and it becomes invincible, not only in the field, but under physical obstacles which seem too onerous for humanity.

The few days that had already passed of this short campaign had all told upon this splendid temper, and the days of preparation for what we regarded as the final struggle for Kimberley by no means served to restore it. The Boers throughout the war proved as clever tacticians as they were feeble strategists. Having wholly failed to grasp the broad issues of the campaign and the vital points to which they should have bent all their energies; having fribbled away their opportunities by besieging Mafeking, Kimberley, and Ladysmith when they ought merely to have veiled the garrisons of those places, and seized the important points of the railway line lying so long defenceless at their feet, even if they did not push their advance to the very seaports themselves; having, in fact, on the broad plan of the war failed as signally as our military authorities at least expected them to fail, they nevertheless on the narrower field of actual warfare displayed a skill which was wholly unexpected.

The Boer commander before Kimberley was now the redoubtable Piet Cronje, who had arrived and assumed command on Monday, November 27. Realising Methuen's weakness in cavalry he masked our whole front with Boer patrols, and confined the finest division in the British army practically to the limits of its own camp. Unconcernedly he moved his supplies in slow and cumbrous bullock wagons across our right front, in full view of our camp, and almost within rifle range. He was safe from our guns, for our ammunition was almost as precious as its equivalent weight in gold, and we were then so ill equipped with weapons of an efficient pattern that we had not even a fuse capable of accurately bursting a shell at a range much in excess of the actual firing range of the Boer Mauser.

In vain Pole-Carew implored that he might be permitted to make a dash on Jacobsdal, which was the Boer base for stores, and which our passage of the Modder seemed to have uncovered and laid at our mercy. So the transport of stores went on unchecked; nay, we began to assume a defensive attitude.

The ground our patrols covered became more circumscribed, and on December 6 some of them fell into Boer ambushes. Notably one under Lieutenant Tristram of the 12th Lancers, which was ambushed near the Riet River, and lost two men killed and two prisoners, including Tristram, who, turning back to rescue one of his men, had his horse shot, and was himself wounded, but nevertheless emptied his revolver, killing one and wounding one Boer, and being finally captured with no less than seven wounds.

One feels that he wears worthily the name of Tristram.

Midnight brought news that Cronje was developing a move from his left front, and that there was ground for uneasiness as to our railway communications, and presently the 12th Lancers received orders to move. Its Lieutenant-Colonel, Lord Airlie, was in command of the expedition, which consisted of the 12th Lancers, the 62nd Battery R.F.A., and five companies of the Argyll and Sutherlands, who were to come out by train, the lancers examining the line ahead; the object of this expedition was to strengthen the post at Enslin (Graspan), held by two companies of the Northamptons, which also proved to be the objective of the Boers, and which is twenty-four miles distant from Modder River Camp.

December 7.—Soon after daylight it became evident that a stiff fight was afoot, and the sound of big guns was presently heard. Lord Airlie's plan was to move down parallel to, and with his right resting on, the railway along which his infantry force was to come; but it soon became manifest that if the small force at Enslin was to be saved he must act without delay, even though the infantry did not arrive. His plan was admirably conceived and executed; pushing steadily forward to cut in between the head of the Boer attack and its line of retreat on Jacobsdal, with the immediate effect of relieving the garrison, for the big gun (there proved to be only one) promptly drew off, followed quickly by the main attack, which found itself in danger of being hemmed in between the garrison and Lord Airlie's little force, and which retired sullenly through a line of *kopjes*, fighting each one until our guns came into action upon it, when the Boer force fell back on the next.

The damage to the railway line fortunately was not very extensive, for the enemy had made certain of taking the station, and indeed the garrison had been hardly pressed, and the defence could not have been greatly prolonged, as the enemy had been able to take ground from which they could rake with rifle fire every side of the small compound, and with their shrapnel they had completely wrecked the little house which was used as a hospital, and in which fourteen of our men were lying wounded.

But for one company having been placed on a stony hill overlooking the station the defence could not have been so long maintained, and great credit is due to Captain Godley in charge of the post; whilst his men behaved splendidly. Lord Airlie's casualties were slight, Lieutenant Wright and one trooper of the 12th Lancers, neither severely wounded, and this although they attacked a force numerically superior, and holding the same ground that Methuen's division had to fight a hard battle to win.

Lord Airlie dislodged the enemy with complete success by moving round to his rear whilst shelling his position, and concluded the fighting before the Argylls had got up, who had been intended to catch the Boer flank as it vacated the *kopjes*.

One Boer severely wounded fell into our hands, and thirteen dead were found and buried, but their wounded were carried off with them. This engagement absolutely discouraged them from any further attempt on the line, and even after Magersfontein, though from Jacobsdal there was an easy descent upon it, the experience of December 7th was a sufficient deterrent.

CHAPTER 4

Magersfontein

Meantime the deviation of rail to cross the Modder River by a low-level bridge had been completed, and on the same day, December 7th, traffic on the north bank was re-established, thereby enabling the 4.7 naval gun to be brought over and made available for the assault on the Spytfontein position, for which preparations were now being pushed forward. A good deal of speculation was rife as to the force and disposition of the enemy, and one could only hope that the actual position was better known to the general than was apparent from what was known by the divisional commanders.

No reconnaissance however was made, nor demonstration of any kind, and one had a feeling of being aboard a ship in shallow waters and in a fog, from which no soundings were being taken.

On Saturday, December 9, the 4.7 gun was moved out before dawn to a ridge about a mile beyond the camp, and at 4.20 a.m. with the first greyness of dawn it sent a shell screaming into the easternmost end of the Langenberg range, and one shell was sent clean over. The range was given at from 7200 to 7600 yards. Watching the firing one did not form the impression that any serious damage was done; there was no visible mark to fire at; but the Boers were quickly moving, and we could distinguish them through our glasses hurrying up to the ridge, where they clustered and watched the proceedings. A horse battery had also come up to join the division, and two of its guns moved to our left front, and joined the chorus (the first horse guns fired in the war) at a range of 4000 yards, opening fire at 5.15 a.m.

By 7 a.m., however, all was over, and troops were back in camp.

In the afternoon Lord Airlie rode out to have a personal inspection of the ground, inviting me to accompany him; and a better opportunity was afforded of noting the consequences of the morning's work. There was no sign of any damage to the Boer position; the trenches were well screened, and were still invisible, but there was a very lively movement going on; from our left towards the right there was a stream of wagons and carts, and mounted men, shifting ground to strengthen the Boer left wing, which our gunfire had revealed as the point of our attack.

A *kaffir* servant came in during the day, having taken advantage of the confusion prevailing in the morning to escape. He stated that the effect of the lyddite shells was terrific, and had created great alarm; he had seen only one man killed, however, and one wounded.

On Sunday, at noon, the advance commenced, and at 3.55 p.m. the 4.7 gun again opened from its position of Saturday morning, supported by a howitzer battery drawn up to within 2500 yards of the base of the *kopjes*, and by a horse and field battery on the right. The bombardment continued until dusk, and had an attack been pushed home that evening there is ground for believing a different result might have been attained, as the heavy bombardment created great alarm amongst the Boers, and one large commando actually moved off. The first experience of lyddite undoubtedly caused a panic, though, owing to the clever entrenchment, and the scattered formation of the enemy, less actual loss was inflicted than might have been expected from so searching a fire.

The Highland Brigade, 9th Lancers, and guns bivouacked about three miles short of the Magersfontein *kopje*; the Guards and 9th Brigade rather nearer camp.

The day had been oppressively hot, and closed in with mutterings of thunder, and towards midnight a storm broke, and the early hours of the day were bitterly cold.

Moving off soon after midnight, General Wauchope led the assault with the Highlanders, in formation of quarter-column, following the directions given by Lord Methuen. What really passed in regard to this form of advance will never be known; certain it is that Wauchope was an enthusiastic supporter of open-order formation, but doubtless he acquiesced in Lord Methuen's desire that the advance should be conducted in close order until within striking distance, in order that a solid and weighty assault should be ensured; and the men were to be deployed when actually within striking distance.

Could any means have been adopted for ensuring the right moment and the right distance for effecting this change of formation, it is evident the advantages of both methods would have been secured, but, alas, the judging of one's whereabouts and the distance travelled on the most familiar ground is very difficult in inky darkness, and on strange ground is a mere matter of luck.

Running across the Boer front, about 400 yards distant from the advanced trenches, was a wire boundary fence, and the Highland Brigade had stumbled into this fence whilst they thought themselves still a mile distant from the Boers. The wire acted like a burglar's alarm, denoting the actual position and distance of our unhappy brigade, into which a withering volley was fired with absolute accuracy, despite the pitch darkness.

Wauchope himself was shot dead, and nearly all the senior officers of the three regiments in advance were either killed or wounded. As an attack the battle was already over. At 5 a.m. our guns opened, and about half-an-hour later the balloon was able to be sent up. One cannot but regret that the action had not been delayed until after the enemy's position had been reconnoitred by means of the balloon, which had just arrived and was equipped with feverish haste, but twenty-four hours too late to do us this most effective service.

The Guards and Yorkshires on our right now found themselves checked by a very heavy fire delivered from trenches on the Modder River bank, which covers the Magersfontein ko-

"Joe Chamberlain" at Modder firing
at the Magersfoniein position.

pjes on their south-east front. The 75th Field Battery gallantly moved forward to a ridge 1100 yards from the Boer position, where, though subjected to a terrific fire, they held on all day, just screened from the worst of the fire by taking advantage of a slight fold in the ground on the ridge top.

But the Boers now began an advance from the trenches strongly held on their left, pushing back the remnants of the Highlanders before them, and at 5.30 a.m. the situation was wearing a very ominous aspect, and a leader of average ability must have inflicted a disastrous defeat on our arms.

At this juncture Brigadier-General Babington, finding the command had devolved upon him, sent out two squadrons of the 12th Lancers dismounted, to try and make good the broken centre. This sounds rather a desperate resource, but the moment was critical—the Boers had pressed steadily on to within 400 yards of the battery, and the attempts to rally the remnants of the Highlanders, who were without officers or even sergeants, proved of no avail; but gallant Lord Airlie pushed through them with his 220 men, and steadily repulsed the Boers into their trenches.

Lieutenant M'Naughten, with the 12th Maxim, behaved with especial gallantry, pushing forward on the most exposed wing, and using the gun with great effect, finally having to bring it out of action by hand, after losing all his horses. Not till 3.45 p.m. were these two squadrons relieved, when the Coldstreams were at length brought up, and took up the ground the 12th had won and held since ten hours before.

The adaptability of these troopers was really remarkable; they adopted the Boer's method of creeping from bush to bush as if by instinct, and proved better at the game than he by reason of their resolution at it.

It was a striking contrast to watch their steady and successful advance, and compare it with the futile rushes from bush to bush of our infantry, who went down in numbers at every onset.

The action had now degenerated into a bombardment on our part, and a desultory rifle fire on the part of the Boers, for not a single gun had so far been fired by them.

The day had grown fiercely hot, and our men were suffering from physical exhaustion, which had time to make itself felt in this lull. There was not a drop of moisture left of all that excess which had made the night so miserable, and the water-bottles, with which men had started about noon the previous day, had, with the true improvidence of the soldier, been mostly emptied the preceding evening, whilst there had been no provision for refilling.

Towards 4 p.m. the Highlanders began to gather together, clearly meditating a final attack, though still no orders were issued, nor was any display made of that capacity which marks the great general, who, by some sharp change of plan, snatches victory in the very teeth of disaster.

The regiments were gathering more from the instinct of the disciplined soldier than from any effort on the part of their officers, of whom indeed very few, and those chiefly subalterns, remained.

The mustering was screened from the Boers by a line of straggling bushes, and the moment of attack was only delayed for a water-cart, which was being brought up to enable the men to moisten their parched lips. This approached without molestation from the enemy, and our men, allowed to fill water-bottles, were in a prolonged queue, taking their turn at the tap, when from near the top of the central *kopje* there was a puff of grey smoke, the scream of a shell, and a big shrapnel fell fortunately just a few yards too far. It was now 4.30 p.m., and this was the first gun fired by the Boers during the day. The effect was magical; the men, wearied and overdone, shaken by the decimation of the morning, simply melted away, and the efforts of the few officers, and the rally of the pipes, were alike vain to stem the retreat. The Boers dropped only two shells into this part of the field, and then turned the gun on to the 9th and 12th Lancers, who were halted and dismounted in a fold of the ground sheltered from all rifle fire, but lying open to this gun fired from a great elevation.

Both regiments suffered some loss from these shells before getting into fresh ground, but though the infantry had thus been swept off the field, and the cavalry forced to change position, our guns never budged, but maintained a fierce bombardment of the enemy's position, whilst the cavalry, in moving out of range of shell, had advanced rather nearer the Boer right wing. To this, doubtless, must be ascribed the immunity enjoyed by the Highlanders in getting off unhampered, but there is no room for doubt that had the Boers promptly advanced in pursuit of them, the day would have ended in complete disaster to the British arms. No such movement, however, was attempted, and night fell, leaving us in the occupation of the positions we had been fighting from during the day.

It is difficult to estimate the extent of the Boer loss; the Highlanders in the early morning had charged down the Scandinavian outpost, about ninety strong, which had been completely overwhelmed, and only five wounded prisoners are believed to have survived, but with this exception the enemy was all day invisible. The best ground for believing they suffered severely is the fact that no effort was made to harass the retiring Highlanders, though the ground was completely favourable for so doing, and sufficiently bushy and broken to be screened from the action of our small band of cavalry.

We even half hoped that the enemy was so shaken that he would abandon the position. At 4.25, however, on the morning of December 12, the armoured train moving out towards Spytfontein Station rudely dispelled any such ideas, for it met such a reception as drove it back incontinently within our lines.

Orders were then issued for a retirement to the Modder River Camp, but Major-General Colville, coming in from his command on the right wing, induced their suspension until a reconnaissance in this direction was found not to encourage the hope of forcing a passage along the valley of the Modder in the then condition of our forces, and our retirement commenced, unmolested except for the Boer artillery, which was quite innocuous, though vigorously shelling the retirement.

The story of the few prisoners taken hardly confirmed the current tales of an impregnable entrenchment of Magersfontein, for, according to them, the Boers had expected us to force the defile through which the railway passed, and only began to move their guns to their left flank after we had shelled that part of the position on Saturday morning.

Attention was now turned towards making the Modder Camp secure whilst reinforcements were gathering, and a tedious and dispiriting pause ensued, accentuated by the unwelcome news which began to trickle in from other quarters. We first learnt that Gatacre, operating from the base resting on East London, had met a very serious reverse in attacking the Stormberg, and as further particulars came to hand the gravity of this news increased, while to blacken still more the outlook the blunt despatch from the commander-in-chief was allowed to appear, announcing a heavy repulse at Colenso (Natal) in the attempt to relieve Ladysmith, with the loss of two batteries.

At every point of our advance then, save the comparatively unimportant one of French's operations before Colesberg, we had met a distinct reverse, and our finest and most seasoned troops had been brought to a stand- still. Nevertheless, the morale of our men never sank. Even the rank and file asked themselves how it was going to be done, and who was going to do it, but that we were going to conquer the Transvaal, occupy Pretoria, and incidentally relieve the beleaguered garrisons at Kimberley, Lady smith, and Mafeking, was never doubted, provided those garrisons could escape famine and pestilence. But it was obvious that no hasty blow must be struck, that we must gather strength, so that whenever we made a fresh start there might be no check.

Meantime the unceasing traffic of a large camp ground the fine sand to powdered dust; parching heat prevailed day after day, and the deadly monotony of the *karoo veldt* ate into our souls, burning with anxiety at least to push the Boer out of British territory and open up the road into Kimberley and Mafeking.

Fortunately we were camped on the river, and though the

stream left much to be desired, it not only afforded a sufficient water supply for all purposes, but admitted of bathing and swimming. This alleviation of the dreadful dust and heat probably did as much as anything to maintain the health and spirits of the men, though it must not be forgotten that the commissariat was most admirably and amply supplied. There was, indeed, no shortfall of anything save gun ammunition.

CHAPTER 5

Rensburg And Grassy Hill

Meantime General French had been slowly gathering a sufficient strength to enable him at the end of December to move. Naturally the chief call for such troops as had arrived in South Africa had been elsewhere than to Colesberg, a country of such natural difficulty that it was recognised that to force a passage of the Orange River in this neighbourhood was a well-nigh impossible task, and to hold the line of communication when forced would in itself require an army corps. Nevertheless it was necessary to push the Boers back from the important railway junction Nauwport, to which they had advanced so close as to blow up a bridge within three-quarters of a mile of the junction, and they were in force at Rensburg, a strong position, only thirty miles distant, whilst they occupied the colonial town of Colesberg.

By the early part of December French was ready with a small and compact force chiefly of cavalry, which he pushed out so effectually that the Boers abandoned Arundel and a number of excellent positions and a carefully prepared *laager* at Taaiboschlaagte after very small resistance, although the operations were not completed till December 30th, at which date the enemy was pushed back into his lines covering the town of Colesberg. Late the following day, advancing his left towards Colesberg, French occupied Maeder's farm, clearing out the Boers from various *laagers* at Vaal Kop and adjacent hills which had been prepared with great care, but which were relinquished under the compelling influence of his flank movements with very slight resistance. On this day the infantry were pushed forward by wagon transport, thus coming on to the debatable ground fresh for action, and the success of the operation was partly due to this fact.

The Berkshires, set down from their wagons, made a dash for a hill in the early dawn, and occupied it before the enemy, taken completely by surprise, was quite aware what was afoot. This hill, afterwards known as M'Cracken's, dominated the Boer position before Colesberg, and lay within four hundred yards of their main trenches, isolated from them by a narrow valley; and for a whole month the Berkshires held this hill under fire every hour of daylight, but quite holding their own, and indeed growing more expert at the sniping game than the Boers themselves. Not a pound of stores could be taken to them by daylight, for the plain behind this hill was commanded from both flanks by rifle as well as gun fire, nor was there any water supply, and everything had to be taken them by night by mule-cart across the plain.

French's New Year greeting to the enemy, however polite in intention, had been certainly very inconvenient. On January 2, as M'Cracken's Hill was found to be a sort of *cul de sac*, or rather a promontory leading nowhere, it would have been abandoned, but that the operation could not be performed in daylight; and as the day's experience proved that it could be held successfully without necessarily entailing loss, whilst its possession completely penned the Boer right, it was resolved not to relinquish it. Our left was therefore strengthened by the Suffolks, established still farther west, and Cole's Kop, a high conical peak overlooking the whole country, but regarded as practically inaccessible for troops, fell into our hands.

Schoeman by this time had found himself so circumscribed that he attempted a relieving movement, but at once encountering the Carabineers (6th Dragoons) and Rimington's Scouts on our extreme right he was easily and quickly repulsed, and the day strengthened the Boers' growing conviction of the ubiquity of French, a conviction which largely conduced to the successful holding of an exterior and very extended line with a numerically inferior force.

But even here all was not to go smoothly. Colonel Watson of the Suffolks had formed the opinion that the Boers would find Colesberg absolutely untenable if a hill known as Grassy Hill were in our possession, and he begged permission to make a night attack upon it, to which, despite the success of New Year's night, General French was not well disposed.

However, Watson returned to the subject, and having inspected the ground in his front, and examined Grassy Hill thoroughly through his glasses, he sent a fresh request to French through Colonel Eustace, R.A., who had visited our left to arrange his guns. French received this renewed request late in the evening, and reluctantly yielded to Colonel Watson's urgency. The desired assent, which was at once telephoned to the Suffolk camp, some eight miles distant on our left wing, reached Colonel Watson at 9 p.m. Arrangements were at once commenced, every precaution was taken, the men were shod as far as possible in canvas shoes to diminish the risk of giving the enemy warning that any move was afoot, and boots were entirely discarded.

At 11.30 p.m. four companies marched out, and advanced over ground that in the darkness at least proved very formidable—men stumbling and falling over big stones and boulders, but nevertheless advancing steadily, though with frequent halts. An idea prevailed that the movement had been signalled to the enemy by some Boer spy (of which every British camp seemed to contain a number); but it is more likely that the sound of motion which inevitably accompanies the movement of a body of men betrayed what was astir. The half battalion having reached the crest of the hill in close order, the colonel and adjutant went forward a few yards to reconnoitre. Suddenly there was a whistle, a lamp was flashed, and instantly there was a crashing volley; the colonel, the adjutant, and three officers were shot dead, and four others wounded, and a number of men were killed and wounded.

"Retire" was heard, and the men persist in saying it was one of the Boers who gave the word, and two companies did retire in good order; the two advance companies, however, attempted to carry the position. Brett on the right succeeded in deploying his men, and charged up to the Boer lines; but was beaten back by a merciless fire, surrounded, and forced to surrender. Our loss amounted to Colonel Watson and four officers killed, four wounded, three prisoners; and twenty-five men killed and 113 prisoners, of whom forty-five were wounded. Happily this mishap did not jeopardise the disposition of French's force, though it probably stayed the evacuation of Colesberg by the Boers.

CHAPTER 6

Among the Frowning Heights

The Household Cavalry which now arrived from England came in contact with the enemy for the first time on January 7, and reinforcements for the Boers began also to arrive— French's activity having caused them anxiety as to whether the line of the Vaal would not be forced at this point, an anxiety still further increased by the seizure of the Slingersfontein chain of hills by Colonel Porter on the 9th.

The Boers were now, however, in sufficient force to hold both wings against the very modest strength at General French's disposal; a reconnaissance on the 11th in some strength on our right evoked stubborn resistance, and the intention to work round to the main line of railway between Colesberg and Norval's Pont was frustrated, although Major Hunter Weston with a small escort managed to push down to near Achtertang to find the Boer reserve stores there strongly guarded and the bridge intact.

Simultaneously with this movement De Lisle moved on our extreme left, pushing down to near the Vaal River on the old wagon road; but here too the enemy was found in considerable force, and the day disclosed the fact that Schoeman was now strong enough numerically to hold the whole line of his defence, some twelve miles, against any concentration French's force was capable of. Obviously then he should have been prompt to take the offensive in his turn, and had he done so our very extended front must at least have been contracted, for our exterior line, containing a Boer force of not less than 3500 men, was quite thirty miles in length, following the semicircular track by which supplies were sent, French's force being of barely equal strength.

However, by way of finding Commandant Schoeman fresh food for thought, a 12-inch gun of 4th Battery R.F.A., under Major Butcher, had been hauled up on the top of Cole's Kop, and was dropping shells on to Grassy Hill at a range of 5100 yards, and into the main *laager* at 5350 yards, whilst the town itself, though full of Boers and lying at the gun's mercy, was respected. The loss at their main *laager* must have been considerable, even though at such range we had no reliable time fuses, and the bursting of shrapnel was therefore a matter of chance. Nevertheless the enemy took advantage of the darkness when it came, not only to remove his tents and stores from the main *laager*, but also to shift some more distant and smaller camps to a point completely out of range.

On the 13th Schoeman gave us a taste of our own physic, for about midday Porter's camp at Slingersfontein was suddenly startled by having some shells from a long-range Boer gun dropped fairly into it, but though the shells were very accurately pitched, no loss was inflicted among men or horses, and the gun was quickly driven off by O Battery R.H.A. However this flank caused Schoeman great anxiety, and on the following night he moved out a force to endeavour to clear the range and force back Porter.

The contrast between the Boer method of night attack and the English comes out clearly in this affair: the Boer merely takes position under cover of darkness, as near as he can get to the point to be assailed, and lies hidden there till the moment is come for his attack. We, on the other hand, always endeavour to drive our attack home. Neither method commands such uniformity of result that it can be either absolutely approved or absolutely condemned, but it would be interesting if some experiments could be made by us in the Boer method.

On this special occasion a party had established itself in a *donga* quite adjacent to our advanced picket held by the Yorks, and lay quite unsuspected till about 10 a.m., when the alertness of our people might be supposed to be somewhat relaxed. Crawling up, they were within a few yards of the breastwork when the sergeant in charge of the picket heard a sound, and looking over a small stone breastwork was instantly shot dead; at the same moment Captain Orr in charge fell badly wounded, and about ten men were down, and the post would certainly have fallen, but that Captain Maddox of the New Zealanders dashed among the bewildered men, and shouting an order to fix bayonets led over the wall on to the no less surprised Boers, who instantly broke and fled, coming under the rifles of the neighbouring picket in doing so, and losing in the encounter thirty-seven men killed.

General French had troops paraded the following day, highly praising the conduct of the New Zealanders and Yorkshires, and naming Captain Maddox. Our loss was seven killed and six wounded.

This day was to be marked, however, with a Boer success. A strong reconnaissance had moved out on Sunday afternoon on our extreme right, in which direction an Australian patrol moved the following morning. Being in touch with the larger body it was rashly assumed that the line of retirement need not be held, and the Boers profited by this to seize two *kopjes* between which the Australian Horse had to retire, and met them in the retirement with a volley from one *kopje* which drove them back on the other, where they were quickly overpowered.

The need for strict observance of the rules of war is repeatedly being rubbed into us by these mere hunters, who probably have never so much as read the history of a campaign, but who, having perfected the art of venery under the stress of hunger, go to the very root of the art of war, and prove most formidable enemies.

The advantages the Boers enjoy, too, of knowing every foot of ground in the whole country is inestimable; not a path or ford or short cut but is known to them, and every move made by us, every arrival of troops or change of disposition is immediately disclosed, for the whole population of the countryside is either Dutch or intermarried with the Dutch, and even the natives, through speaking the language and living with the people, are assuredly more useful vehicles of information to the Boers than to the British.

Despite these advantages, despite a slight superiority in numbers, and the possession of interior lines, we were penning Commandant Schoeman more and more closely, and the arrival of General Clements with portions of an infantry brigade led us to believe that we might at least wrest the town of Colesberg from the enemy, though any idea of a regular advance into the Orange Free State on this line seemed more and more preposterous as we gained greater command of the surrounding country and realised its nature.

From Rensburg to Norval's Pont, where the main line crosses the river, is a distance of about thirty-five miles, the elevation falling by about five hundred feet, and the whole country being broken by steep stony *kopjes* and deep valleys. Nowhere is there a valley wide enough for the unhampered movement of troops, much less one that is not completely commanded from the surrounding hills by rifle fire, not to speak of artillery, which the Boers showed a perfectly marvellous power of moving on and among these frowning hills.

Despite all this French had curled round the Boer left flank, and had reached so near to the main line of railway and to the large Boer depot near Achtertang that Schoeman was making daily but ineffective efforts to push him back, and we began to look upon the reoccupation of Colesberg as an imminent event.

January 22, the anniversary of Isandhlwana twenty-one years ago, showed little enough in the outlook to relieve the gloom which had settled on the country since that fatal week in early December of the past year, though assuredly there was anything but gloom amongst the troops at and around Rensburg, and the spirit prevailing there may be illustrated by an incident which was enacted at this time.

The countryside is a favourite haunt for game, and of the antelope tribe, once in such countless herds throughout the country, there are still hereabouts a goodly number of springbok, as the skins to be found in the abandoned Boer *laagers* amply testified. Nor were our own people averse to varying the monotony of a campaign by a little hunting when chance offered. The officer acting as remount with General French at this period was Lieutenant Burt, 3rd Dragoon Guards, a tireless and zealous gatherer of any herds of horses roaming the veldt, though little enough he took for his pains, the enemy having commandeered every horse in the country fit to carry a man. Taking a holiday one afternoon. Lieutenant Burt, accompanied only by his soldier servant, went a-hunting.

Though *bok* was fairly numerous in any direction, none of course could have the delicacy of flavour of those feeding near the Boer *laager*, and accordingly the intrepid sportsman turned his horse's head in that direction, and after some fruitless shots knocked over a buck within a couple of miles of the Boer position. As he dismounted to give it the *coup de grace* his servant, who was mounted and holding his master's horse, reported that there were some mounted Boers moving near them.

Looking up, Burt saw four or five men "riding-in" a troop of ponies which had been grazing near them hidden by a fold in the ground, and remarking, "Dash it! Charles, that's my job," he jumped on to his horse and galloped for the nearest Boer, who dismounted and fired, but missed. Charles discovered another Boer on their flank, hitherto hidden by the same fold of the ground, and shouted a warning to his master, who swept round at a gallop and rode straight at the newcomer; he, not having time to dismount, fired from his saddle, but failed to stop our dragoon, who promptly knocked up his gun and had him by the collar.

Threatening to shoot him if he offered resistance, Burt forced the unwilling Dutchman in front of him back towards Rensburg, after handing the Mauser to his servant, and though a rescue party hurried out, by keeping in the open plain the captive was brought, sulky and unwilling, a prisoner to French's camp. Before they got in the servant's horse had been knocked over by a bullet through the thigh, but the gallant beast had been got up and had brought his rider into camp.

Burt himself had his rifle knocked out of his hand by a bullet, but he halted his prisoner and handed him over to the faithful Charles on the wounded horse, whilst he dismounted and re-covered it. A mad escapade, say you? Well, perhaps so, but thank God we have gallant youngsters to do mad things, and thereby possess such fighting stuff that we are occupying the enemy's positions when we ought, by the rules of the game, to be running away. As long as we have got such officers, so long shall we have such soldiers.

Captain Lawrence found the prisoner little good as a source of information, for he was so sorely wounded in temper that he not only wouldn't talk, but wouldn't even eat until a night's reflection had restored appetite, if not communicativeness.

This same day we heard that Major Haig, who had through all the war been with General French from the first days in Natal and in all the well-devised and well-executed operations that had pushed the Boers back from threatening Nauwport almost to the banks of the Orange River, was to be relieved.

General French, not the least of whose high qualities is to know the value of his fellow-men, wired to the commander-in-chief begging that he might retain the services of Major Haig as D.A.A.G., and received a reply fully recognising the great merits of that officer and appreciating his desire to keep him, but adding that since the command had reached such dimensions it was necessary that the D.A.A.G. should hold corresponding rank. Oh admirable regulations! Long may you survive to neutralise the value even of brilliant service! and continue to thrust round men into square holes. But for these glorious regulations what should we do with the poor round men?

Luckily, however, Lord Roberts is a strong man as well as a wise one, and so, though superseded, Major Haig never left the staff; nay he even kept the strings of his work between his fingers, the new man conniving with the fiction of a change. A few weeks brought Haig an exceedingly well-earned step, and he thereupon resumed nominally the work he had never, in fact, relinquished.

Meantime, French had been called to Cape Town to state what he proposed to do with the reinforcements he had been asking for if he had them. His frank avowal that there was no room for any operations more considerable than the reoccupation of an inconsiderable upcountry township, and the pushing the invaders back to within their own border, may have cost him some pangs, as it might condemn him to an inglorious inactivity. Anyhow, the avowal was unhesitatingly made, and whether *propter hoc* or merely *post hoc*, he came back to Rensburg named for the command of cavalry in the advance for the relief of Kimberley.

One incident of these days deserves to be recorded as illustrating the use made by the Boers of their guns. On February 1st our people on the summit of Cole's Kop were astonished by a shell from a Vickers-Maxim being thrown over their heads. Neither it nor any subsequent shell did the slightest damage, but the fact that the Boers succeeded in pitching a shell over our position at a considerably greater elevation than their own, and at a distance of certainly 5000 yards from a gun whose limit of range was supposed to be not much over 3000 yards, is quite deserving of notice.

And it is worth considering in this connection whether our plan is sound, of estimating the value of gunfire so completely by effectiveness of destruction. Is it not possible that there is a certain effectiveness of disturbance in what is regarded as ineffectual gunfire, which is of greater value than we always attach to it.

It may be that the harmlessness of the Boer fire may, now that the war is drawing to an end, lead us to belittle the effects of their shell-fire at impossible ranges, and because we suffered few casualties, thereby to forget the vexatious delays which were thus forced upon our troops, and which often enabled an un-hampered Boer retreat when the situation appeared hopeless for them.

The unwillingness to fight our guns in sections of batter-ies seems, too, a point requiring reconsideration. The objection often heard that it is desirable to concentrate fire on the enemy is of course absurd; fire can be better concentrated from sev-eral points against the same spot, than from one point. That the equipment and drill of a battery makes six guns the most con-venient unit is also not an admissible objection; reform needs to be aimed at that particular fact, and facility of subdivision of batteries would often be found of very great and unmistakable advantage. Possibly our guns at Colenso would never have been lost but for our habit of sticking them up in a row to form a conspicuous target.

CHAPTER 7

Masterly Tactics of French

It is difficult to over-estimate the importance of the operations round Colesberg, and the great influence they exercised over the progress of the campaign. Judged by the standard of apparent results, or theatrical effect, there is little enough to rivet the attention. Nevertheless they deserve and will repay review. First they are notable as being the one point where the British arms maintained an unbroken superiority. From Natal on the east, following the semicircle right round to Mafeking on the west, at no point save this was there a glimmer of success.

It had come to be feared not only that we could barely hope to save Mafeking, but that Ladysmith with its 13,000 troops must fall. Buller had been repulsed repeatedly. Gatacre had been unsuccessful, Methuen had been beaten to a standstill, and at this one point only did fortune smile. What were the conditions then which made this part of the campaign such a notable exception. Had we a great superiority of numbers? Was the country especially favourable for the operations of our troops? Or was the fighting capacity of Schoeman's commando inferior?

As for numbers there seems to have been no very great disparity until late in January, when the advantage always held by the Boers became more pronounced.

As for the configuration of the country, it was infinitely worse even than the line of the Tugela, from Colesberg, right back to the Orange River. Tremendously broken, with stony, wooded *kopjes*, separated by narrow valleys, with marsh or donga in the bottoms. Difficult for any troops; exceeding difficult for cavalry.

And as for fighting qualities, Schoeman's men were nearly all Free-Staters, who have proved themselves the most stubborn fighters of the Boer armies.

One is driven back, therefore, to the conclusion that only to a difference in the method of handling his troops can General French's success be ascribed. The very absence of any striking achievement is indeed the salient fact of the movement. Never was there a pitched battle. If the Boers held any position in force and meant showing fight, French played with them in front whilst he sent a force round the corner, so entrenched camp after entrenched camp was abandoned with hardly a struggle, and whilst everywhere else the Boers were pushing farther and farther into British territory, at this point they were being pushed steadily back.

The Boer estimate of French was shown then as it has been shown since; there is no man, not even the little field-marshal, who has been so often killed in Boer despatches. But two unsolicited testimonials were given at that time. The first was by three Boers who were taken prisoners on 20th January, and who accounted for their sorry plight by saying that both men and horses were starved and worn-out by endless marchings and counter-marchings; they were always on the move—no time to eat, to sleep, to rest.

They never knew where French was, or what he was up to; in the morning sweeping round his right to threaten the main line of railway down by Achtertang, and in the afternoon seizing the old wagon road thirty miles away, and the Boers were forever galloping from one extremity of their line to the other, but they could never either delude or force him into a real fight; he just worried them.

Ten days later I was in Cradock, a prosperous agricultural town about midway between the Orange River and Port Elizabeth, and met there a certain Mr. Armstrong, who was very curious to learn from me the truth as to French's operations. Asking him for a reason for such special curiosity as he was displaying,

A Lancer Patrol with Captured Boers

he gave me this explanation, which certainly does not lose force in view of the very disturbed state of the Cape Colony in November 1900, when the chances of the struggle had completely reversed themselves. This is what he said:—

> A few days since my son brought me a message from a well-to-do Dutch farmer in this district, advising me to send away any valuable movables I might have, without delay. I made it my business to see the man, who had a real regard for me in return for good offices done in the past and a hunting comradeship, and asked what he meant.
>
> With great precautions as to secrecy he told me that a rising of the Dutch in the Cradock district was arranged, and was imminent. I asked contemptuously 'what they were waiting for; could their cause ever look more hopeful?' and he answered quite seriously that if only some disaster should befall French the whole district would be ablaze.

It was an insurrection that never became complete.

Round Colesberg on a small scale the plan was being tried with complete success that was so shortly to be applied by the field-marshal on the grand scale, and which in a few weeks was to revolutionise the whole course of the war. As it happens, the general, who from comparative obscurity had issued to keep aloft and unrepulsed the ancient banner, was to be selected as the executive arm in the wider field so soon to be opened.

Of course the field-marshal had measured the value of this little campaign; it did not escape him that here was one who, setting at nought the textbooks, was fighting the Boers on the true scientific principle of adapting the knowledge of the past to the needs of the present, meeting arms of great precision and extraordinary effectiveness with scattered formation and ever shifting front, and thereby neutralising the advantages so conspicuously maintained by the Boers at every other point.

To say that Lord Roberts, the veteran commander-in-chief, learnt from French's operations is to credit Lord Roberts with large-minded perceptivity, and his choice of French to lead the relief of Kimberley gives ground for the statement.

Be that as it may, to French and his chief of staff, Haig, belong the credit of having successfully inaugurated and maintained a method of warfare which was to be applied to the whole conduct of the war by our greatest commander, and which was to achieve, within a fortnight of its adoption, the relief of Kimberley and the complete breakup of all the Boer armies at every part of the seat of war.

And what of the men to whom must be accredited the departure from the old methods, and who were to apply the new plan with such unfailing success? That French is a born cavalry leader his achievements throughout the war clearly demonstrate, yet his appearance on a charger by no means prepares one to expect either his own capacity for prolonged occupation of the saddle, or the ease with which his cattle carried him.

Short in stature, and square of build, there is not the least suggestion of an Irishman about him, till you catch, which you very immediately do, a clear grey eye, which looks out at you very frankly and observantly, and which proves capable at times of burning with a lurid fervency which makes the object of its regard inclined to remember pressing engagements elsewhere. No mischance in the operations disturbs its serenity, but any slackness of movement, or slowness of comprehension on the part of an officer entrusted with a critical move in the game will, without fail, kindle the flame.

Of absolute coolness under fire, he is extremely quick in what one might describe as "recovering his game," and is very clever in not only laying out his plan of operations, but in modifying and altering them according to the actual fortunes of the day. A most uncomfortable companion in action, because it never seems to occur to him that if a bullet hits you it generally hurts, and an adept at that most trying of all movements in battle, riding back under fire as steadily as riding up to it.

Undoubtedly one of the secrets of his success was his accessibility. Anybody could get speech of him, and everybody with anything to say was certain of a hearing, and certain, too, that if he said anything valuable use would be made of it.

This capacity to get good men round him, and keep them when he had secured them, was also invaluable, and no abler staff was to be found in the whole campaign; whilst for the D.A.A.G., Major (now Lieutenant-Colonel) Haig, one does not hesitate to predict a very distinguished career.

CHAPTER 8

A New Departure

In the early days of February it became known that all preparations were completed, and that the hour had come when we were to learn whether the skill which had prevailed so mightily against the barbarous Afghans was to prove as effective against the no less barbarous but better armed Boers.

Although the greatest secrecy had been maintained as to all movements of troops, a secrecy so carefully guarded, that a warning from a military medical friend to me, reading, "Come as soon as possible," had not been allowed to pass, though when he had rewritten it to read, "The doctor recommends immediate change of air," it was passed by the censor with a twinkle of appreciation, yet it was recognised very clearly that Methuen s Division was holding open the gate of ingress to the enemy's country.

And the Boers themselves were equally aware of the concentration going on in that direction, yet, by an extraordinary failure to grasp the significance of the situation, they were content to still sit idly round Ladysmith with one large portion of their forces, whilst with the other they were sitting with equal supineness before Kimberley.

Their other detached forces were not ill employed in holding in check considerable forces detailed on our side to maintain intact some vital points in our long lines of communication; but it is a matter for deep wonderment that a renewal of that attack of January 6th on Ladysmith, which had so narrowly escaped success, was not repeated at this later stage, when the condition of the beleaguered had become so much more favourable to an assault, whilst the state of the Boer cause rendered either the overwhelming of Sir G. White, or the pushing back of an extended left arm, a matter of vital moment.

It can hardly be doubted that a determined attack on Ladysmith at any time during the latter half of the month of January or early in February must have met with success. That its gallant defenders would have fought to the last ditch cannot be questioned, but, weakened by disease and diminished supplies of all sorts, the chances were all in favour of the enemy, notwithstanding the presence of Buller's relieving force at Colenso. Such a success was indeed imperatively necessary for the Boer cause; had it been achieved, there was the faint chance that an offer to end the war on some reasonable terms of concession might have been entertained.

Such at least was the one slender chance which a far-sighted Boer leader might have staked all to win. Especially should this card have been played when Spion Kop had demonstrated to him by how narrow a margin was he able to hold his own, with all his entrenchments, against Buller's force alone; and when he tasted the bitterness of defeat, as he must have done in finding himself, after being driven off Spion Kop, under necessity to abandon his positions between it and Ladysmith, and only saved by the astounding ignorance on our part of what had happened, so that we retreated with equal precipitation, and he was able once more to make good his hold.

Then was the moment, if it ever existed at all, to fall with overwhelming fury on Ladysmith and carry it at all hazards whilst its defenders were suffering in the first disappointment of their sanguine hopes.

But even if the renewal of an attack on Ladysmith was impracticable in the memory of the bitter loss previously incurred on January 6th, then the other card, not nearly so promising of success, but still perfectly practicable, might have been played, of shifting 8000 or 10,000 men rapidly across the country by train to Edenburg, reinforcing Cronje and capturing Kimberley, or forcing the English camp at Modder River by throwing a strong commando across its rear from Jacobsdal.

Perhaps the previous successes of the Boer arms were his undoing. Strong in an unshakable belief that the Almighty was on his side, he probably believed that we should continue to march up to his entrenched positions and be mowed down by his murderous fire; that the Lord would continue to deliver us into his hand, in fact, and all he had to do was to sit still and annihilate us when the moment came.

Probably he counted, too, on the fact that the reinforcements which had been pouring into the country for the past two months were not of the seasoned quality of the troops he had already encountered, and had held in check.

Certain it is the days which offered such opportunity as was ever to exist for him were allowed to slip by, and the campaign was about to re-open with all the advantage of offensive operations still attaching to the English commander.

The extraordinary belief in, and love for, the field-marshal entertained by Mr. Thomas Atkins, was a sufficiently powerful force to give stamina and cohesion to the somewhat raw material of which the reinforcements were so largely composed, and actual experience was to show that the troops which had come to South Africa since December were as capable of sustained effort and resolute advance as the most seasoned regiments in the service.

Indeed, one of the most striking features of this war has been the fact that regiments whose past opportunities for distinction have been few, or who have not even seen active service, have during this war repeatedly singled themselves out, and secured a splendid reputation.

And so it came to pass that if Mr. Kruger did rely on having to encounter men who, while more numerous, were so inferior in stamina and courage that their effort would prove even less effectual than that of those he had so far succeeded in keeping at bay, he was quickly to be undeceived. Though, without doubt, had the same method of fighting prevailed, such hopes might have been justified.

My verdict on the reserve man is, however, very different. My opinion of him, gleaned from what I saw in the field, differs wholly from that expressed by politicians in England, and though I cannot pretend to be wholly and exclusively in the right, yet I desire to record my view in order that the bare truth may be ascertained.

Generally, then, I regard the reservist as a snare and a delusion. He is able to give free rein to all the unsoldierly vices of dirt, shirking, disobedience, or that worse quality—half-obedience. He is the man who on the hot toilsome marches loses his rifle; and he is the man to whom, if to any one, is to be traced the sounding of that fatal word "retire," which has led more than once in this very war to some of its least creditable episodes. He is able to do these things, first, because he knows from his past experience that they can be, and are, done; secondly, because there is today absolutely no check upon him. Field punishments, Nos. 1, 2, and 3, are a farcical delusion. Every commanding officer will admit that they are impracticable, at any rate, in the field.

Flogging is no longer permissible, and a bad soldier cannot be ruled by fear. I remember once interposing in a discussion of this subject, and, in a mild and low voice, suggesting that he might be covered with ignominy by being sent to the base. My proposal was received with a shout of laughter. Ignominy, at least of such a nature, was not held to be an effective substitute for the cat.

Then what about the converse method? How about rewards? For the ordinary trooper or private such exist, and one can do something; but for the reservist this is not so. What does a man who, at the end of the campaign, goes back to civilian life, care for such rewards for good conduct in the field as are possible of extension to the ordinary rank and files?

An extra penny per day pension proves a very poor inducement; besides, if he is too keen he may not survive to enjoy it. No! if an officer had to select men for arduous, dangerous, and prolonged effort, there would not be many who would be found to give preference to reservists over raw recruits—there wouldn't be one who would take all reservists, rather than all men of one or more years' service; and most officers are not disposed to welcome a large draft of reservists.

The fact that men flocked to the standards should count for very little in favour of the system of "Reserve," if, when they rejoin, they are found to deserve the character indicated in my paragraph.

CHAPTER 9

Changing Front

On February 7th, General French and his staff passed through Nauwport, *en route* for Modder River railway bridge, and the transference of practically his entire force from before Colesberg commenced, and other regiments and troops came up under Clements' command, enabling the withdrawal of French's Division. Incidentally it may be noted that, within ten days of the change, the Boers, under Schoeman, had resumed the offensive, and pushed Clements right back to Arundel, the first station out of Nauwport, a striking testimony to the value of the Cavalry Division, and of the terror and respect inspired by French.

Tuesday, February 11th, was named as the time of rendezvous; Ramdam was the place. French's Division was to consist of three cavalry brigades—the first, under Colonel Porter, to consist of the Carabineers, the Greys, one squadron of Inniskillings (6th Dragoons), and one of New South Wales Lancers; the second, under Colonel Broadwood, of the Household Cavalry, the 10th Hussars, and 12th Lancers; the third, under Colonel Gordon, of the 9th and 16th Lancers. Two brigades of mounted infantry— the first, under Colonel Hannay, having four battalions; and the second, four battalions also, under Colonel Ridley.

There were seven batteries R.H.A. under Colonel Davidson, but Colonel Eustace, who had been with French all through, re-joined him immediately, taking command of the guns. Attached also was a Pontoon company and one field company of Royal Engineers.

On February 12th, leaving Ramdam, French mustered 4890 sabres.

Tucker's division of infantry was to follow the line of French's advance, and make good the ground for him, whilst Kelly-Kenny's division was to follow along the line of the Modder River. The Guards and the Highland Brigades were held for an intermediate line, or for the support of either division, and Lord Methuen was left with a strong garrison at Modder River railway bridge.

Ramdam is the name of a large artificial lake and farm, owned by a prosperous Boer farmer, just inside the Orange Free State border, due east of Graspan. On Sunday morning, February 11th, its quiet was disturbed by the arrival of Major Rimington with his corps of guides. No opposition whatever was encountered, though the Boers had been at the farm in some strength that morning.

A picture of Rimington that fine autumn morning paints itself for me as I write. "Mike" has been so identified with South Africa that one almost forgets that he, too, hails from "the disthressful country." A tall, well-built soldier, of unsleeping vigilance and keen observation, he had been connected with the collection of information about the country south of the Limpopo River for full twenty years. Up to the very outbreak of the war he had been in the Free State, and was as well known in Bloemfontein as at the Curragh.

Of his vigilance, his escape from Bloemfontein is a sufficient guarantee; he didn't leave it at all with the connivance of Mr. Steyn's government. Coming back to Cape Town, in September 1899, he was at once entrusted with the formation of a corps of guides, intrepid scouts, who knew the country, talked Dutch, rode and shot with skill, and were as tricky as the Boers themselves. Rimington himself was sleepless and watchful, a good judge of a horse, a fine rider, and splendid polo player; cool, wary, and bold, the very man for the work he had undertaken.

Sitting with him on a stony ridge overhanging Ramdam, it was a stirring sight to watch the steady advance of our battalions (the cavalry were coming in from Modder River, fully twenty-five miles distant, and appeared only a cloud of dust on the horizon), and to speculate as to what the hours held for us all. Nay, what the hours held for the Empire, for now we were about to put its fortunes to the touch.

Of course, looking back today, the issue seems unquestionable—the end was sure from the beginning; but sitting on that stony ridge, aware that the Boers were watching the movement even as we were, remembering the frightful havoc which rifle fire does play in these days of repeating Mausers, conscious indeed of what we could ourselves accomplish were the forces we were watching hostile ones, the task had to be judged in the light of events that had passed, and one could but feel that it was no trifling one; that unless the blundering of the past was avoided all our strength of numbers would go for naught, and that the deep-seated jealousy of English power and wealth so universal amongst Continental peoples, would blaze into actual hostility under the fostering influences of continued disaster to the British arms.

I believe this reflection was very vividly shared in the United Services, nevertheless, though the gravity of the situation was recognised, and the magnitude of the task, there was no flinching or hesitancy, and at no period of our history has the real gallantry of our forces more truly and unostentatiously shown itself.

It was a curious sight that quiet Sunday. When the Rimington Guides rode down to the huge pan in the early morning, the water was dotted with wild duck, coot, and moorhens, the sandy marge was alive with waders, but by noon all the wild denizens of the wastes were driven out and their places occupied by the dusty and travel-stained circumstance of war.

Men were shouting and swimming in the pan, horses and mules were trampling knee-deep in the muddy edges, the slopes were dotted with all the shabby lumbersome paraphernalia of a large camp, and infusing all was the intangible feeling of expectation, and withal a cheerful resolution that had been sadly missing for some time.

The day wore on with constant addition to the gathered force, but later it began to be known that the concentration had not passed wholly without a hitch. Colonel Hannay, coming up from Ramah Drift of the Orange River, had been heavily engaged, and had sustained some loss, increased by treachery; a Boer in a clerical dress having led a detachment of our people down to water after the fighting was over, it was surprised by an *ambuscade*. Colonel Porter in command of the 1st Brigade was delayed by this circumstance with the Carabineers, and did not assume his command for some days in consequence, only reaching the division on the evening of the 14th at Klip Drift.

Monday, February 12, at 2 a.m. the cavalry division commenced the advance. Hardly were we clear of the camp when we came in touch with the enemy posted in very broken and mountainous country covering the natural drift of the Riet River. Our first touch of them was dramatic enough; a patrol of Rimingtons under Captain Rankin was sent to occupy a high detached hill on our left; as day was breaking it reached the top to find a much stronger detachment of Boers just establishing itself on the hill; Rankin's patrol of six men, including himself, were instantly driven off, and actually got down with nothing worse than their clothes perforated by Mauser bullets and their leader with a sprained ankle.

With daylight the Boers opened on our advance with two guns, the general and staff receiving a morning salute and having a marvellous escape, as three shells burst right amongst them. French detached a battalion of mounted infantry and a battery of horse guns to amuse the Boers, whilst he pushed forward his main advance unconcernedly.

During this part of the operations a very curious and pretty sight presented itself. The sun had not yet dispelled the heavy morning mist, heralding a very hot day, and the game had not yet sought its daily sanctuary; a large herd of springbok, perhaps some four or five hundred, were therefore caught unawares between the belligerents, and galloped confusedly first into one position, then into another, flashing out from the mist into the sunlight, and anon swallowed again in the rolling vapour, then suddenly dashing on top of a company of mounted infantry posted in some *kopje,* so bewildered by the firing and the number of people as to be utterly unable to get away from the danger, and by no means passing scatheless through the zones of fire.

Meantime the Boers were discovering an entirely changed order of proceeding. No longer was our method, when we discovered them, to attack forthwith, no matter how forbidding the ground, or how easily turned; now, on the contrary, French merely left a screen before them, and passed on as though they were non-existent.

Then was once more manifested the huge importance of mounted troops for a South African war, for pushing steadily on with his right, by 9.15 a.m. we had seized a drift further east than Waterval, and by the speed of our advance were in actual possession by the advance patrol when the Boer left dashed down to contest the passage.

But for Major Hunter Weston, R.E., we might even then have lost the drift, for whilst men and horses were vainly trying to quench the all-devouring thirst of the country, the Boers, hidden by the sharply rising banks, were rapidly approaching, and but that he dashed down at the imminent risk of his neck and the actual loss of his horse, and warned Captain Majendie in command to line the north bank, we should probably have been driven out.

Taking advantage of thick cover, however, the attack was repulsed, after a very hot half-hour, during which Captain Majendie was shot dead, and the passage was made good, a battery being crossed to command the plain on the north bank, and a most excellent start had now been accomplished. The remainder of the day was devoted to crossing the cavalry division and its guns and stores, and preparing for the next step of forcing the Modder River.

I cannot forbear here from introducing a personal anecdote, for it is of wide interest as illustrating the character of the little field-marshal. I had had the misfortune to fall under the displeasure of the press control, in having refused to recognise the right of the commandant at Orange River, to over-ride my various permits granted by men senior to himself, and by pushing forward without waiting for his confirmation of my right to do so. Captain Kenna, V.C., General French's provost, had notified that I must report myself at headquarters this day, and only by his kindness had I been able to be present at the operations, under a solemn undertaking to report in the Modder River Station camp before sunrise next day. Having witnessed the operations, I therefore came sadly back at midday, to Ramdam, to hand in my permits to Captain Kenna, and proceed on the further twenty-five miles to Modder River Camp.

To my surprise, I found Ramdam occupied by the Field-Marshal's staff, and, finding out Lord Stanley, I received a severe reprimand for disregarding any military orders, notwithstanding that they might appear at variance with some previously issued, and was told I could not continue with French's Division. I refused to remain with any other, and was recommended to see King-Hall—the officer in command at Orange River—and get the matter put right, when I could apply for a new permit.

It was only after I had retired from this most unsatisfactory interview that I recollected that there as yet could be no news of the day's operations at headquarters. I therefore again sought Lord Stanley, and, remarking that my being under a cloud need not deprive him of the earliest news, tendered my note-book. Very shortly after he came with Colonel Henderson to obtain as many details as I could give, and this led to my being introduced to Lord Roberts, who, having extracted the last atom of information, asked what I was doing. This is what ensued.

"What are you doing here?"

"I am a sort of prisoner, sir."

"What for?"

Then I explained.

"Where are you going now?"

"To Modder River."

"Modder River! What Modder River?"

"Modder River Camp."

"Now?"

"Yes."

"What, after being in the saddle since midnight and through an engagement? Why are you in such haste?"

"Because, as the price of being present at today's fight, I gave Captain Kenna a promise to be at Modder River Camp before sunrise tomorrow."

"Umph!" Then turning to Lord Stanley: "What can we do for him; he has brought us some very good news?"

Stanley replied, "I think we might give him seventy-two hours to collect his kit"; thus giving an excellent tip of what was to be expected, as well as one for the conclusion of the interview.

"Kit! Where is your kit?"

"At the front, sir."

"What did you leave your kit at the front for?"

"Because I hoped to get back there to rejoin it."

"Oh, let him go, Stanley!"

And I rejoined the cavalry division before midnight; and carried with me a memory that will be cherished through my life, and an understanding why this bright-faced little veteran is the darling of his soldiers, who repose a trust in his military knowledge, based upon his knowledge of, and thought for, his men.

A Cavalry Bivouac

CHAPTER 10

A Brilliant Dash

The confusion of the previous afternoon, when ammunition columns were tumbling over food convoys, and batteries over both, in the effort to get to the north bank of the Riet River, had dropped into the ordered chaos of the passage of a difficult river long before nightfall, and only for a few hours was there any cessation of movement, and at the streak of day the cavalry division was chafing to be "let go." Before the word was given, however, the field-marshal and his staff had visited and inspected the troops, given the latest development of his plans, and returned to watch the infantry advance in support.

At a few minutes past 8 a.m. French set his troops in motion. We well knew that an arduous and even desperate duty lay before us; the march to the Modder River, distant some twenty -four miles, was over a country absolutely without water, save at a single well about half-way, where the supply was wholly inadequate for the men, to say nothing of the horses and mules, and was to be left untouched.

It was the hottest season of the year, and the hottest day of the hot season; the enemy were mustering to oppose our advance, and we should strike the Modder River at Randheuvel Drift, only thirteen miles distant from Cronje's camp at Magersfontein. There was a tolerable certainty, therefore, that we should have a stout resistance offered to our approach to the river.

Hardly had the advance begun than fighting opened on our left flank; but though the enemy was in some strength, our march continued unimpeded. Every half-hour or so a Maxim opened in support of the advanced patrol, which was keeping up a pretty constant exchange of fire; but the enemy was constantly falling back to avoid being enfolded by our centre and right swinging round on him.

Already the day had grown red-hot; the ground, sparsely covered by the scanty *karoo* herbage, was so hot, that we found ourselves shifting from one foot to the other in the frequent halts, to ease our burning feet. The thought of what the poor animals must be suffering was accentuated by the all too frequent sight of a gun-horse dropping in his traces as though he had been shot, or a troop-horse pitching headlong and helpless. It was a heart-breaking spectacle, and our own burning thirst and suffering quickened our sympathies with the dumb animals.

As the day wore on we became certain of one thing, *viz.*, that no army that the Boers could put into the field would hold our men back from the river; nothing short of utter annihilation would accomplish that.

By this time the enemy with whom we had been engaged were completely overlapped; they made an attempt to surprise a squadron of the 16th Lancers which visited a deserted farm on our left in the vain hope of finding water, but failed lamentably. It was surprising to find the farms, lying in the heart of the enemy's country, already not only deserted, but almost stripped of portable valuables; and it was much later that we heard how the Transvaal *burghers*, who had come south to repel the British, had levied toll of stock and chattels upon the unhappy Free Stater who had rushed into the Transvaal quarrel, not only to take all the ordinary risks of war, but even to be robbed and pilfered by his allies.

About 4 p.m. there appeared on the edge of the plain we had now entered a fringe of trees which marked the course of the river, and the day had fallen cool from the gathering of a thunderstorm, which seemed to burst all round, but not overhead. Then came the supreme moment of the day; even the weary horses were no longer tired, but advanced with a dash and resolution which, though it left the guns toiling far in the rear, obviated the need for them by taking the enemy so utterly by surprise that resistance was overpowered before it had time to gather.

It is pretty certain the last half-hour of that toilsome march was not "by the book," but the effort to check the advance and let the guns get up was always modified by the knowledge of how distracting it was to the Boer to find himself in the face of a rapid enveloping attack. So the squadrons dashed on, and the centre was under cover of a detached house with a splendid water supply almost before the Boer camp was awake to its danger. The 12th Lancers, supported by a battalion of Mounted Infantry, dashed through the drift under a dropping fire, with but few casualties, and, leaving the camp to the good care of the main body, successfully pursued, captured, and brought back a number of wagons containing most welcome stores, chiefly of forage.

The right, under Broadwood, had dislodged a Boer outpost, and pursued it to the river on our right, and the day was crowned with a great success. The Boer camp was in our hands, with all its stores, tents, and appurtenances, a good many wagons, and the oxen of the wagons captured by Lord Airlie. The ovens were full of fresh bread, smoking hot, and there was even a considerable supply of luscious fresh fruit, pears, peaches, and grapes. We began to reach the conclusion that the stories of an imperfectly organised Boer commissariat which had prevailed so early as December had very small foundation in fact.

This brilliant dash had established the cavalry division within twenty miles of Kimberley, practically without casualties, and between Cronje and his base.

It is true that, but for the supplies in the Boer camp, we were without fodder for the horses and mules; but the river banks provided some scanty pasturage for the mules, and the captured Boer stores afforded a day's feed for the horses. Still it was obvious we could not move till our supplies came up.

Patrols scoured the country round at daylight, and reported it fairly clear of the enemy, and no large bodies about; nevertheless, the camp sustained a vigorous cannonading in lieu of breakfast, and only after a prolonged artillery duel did Major Burton's battery succeed in driving off the Boer guns, after having twice dismounted one of them. Although the Boer shells had been well directed and burst admirably, we escaped marvellously without loss, except that some horses and mules were knocked over. This was serious enough, seeing that the effects of the heavy work already accomplished, particularly the frightful march of the 13th, had exacted a terrible toll. Forty to sixty horses from a regiment; in some cases all but two or three of the horses of a battery had to be temporarily condemned, and the conditions were not improving, neither was the task growing less arduous.

CHAPTER 11

The Relief of Kimberley

During the night of February 14 the convoy had come in, and Tucker's infantry division, after a magnificent bit of marching over the same waterless waste the cavalry had crossed, arrived with it, making good the line of our advance, and enabling the cavalry division to go forward once more with full nosebags and replenished wallets.

We moved on at 9.45, taking a north- easterly direction, and had not proceeded an hour before we found ourselves in face of a strong Boer force. The Boer centre rested on a lofty and thickly-bushed square *kopje*, his left resting on the river and strongly posted in broken and wooded ground extending from his centre to the river banks; his right was projected into the plain, holding an advanced ridge at right angles to the main position, and overlapping the British left. Three guns (Krupps) were posted along this ridge.

A heavy rifle fire pushed back our patrol only after our main advance was distant little more than a mile from the Boer main position, the Boers having waited with the utmost confidence until we were well into the jaws of the trap; rifle bullets were kicking up the dust pretty sharply amongst us, when two batteries, T and U, drew out and unlimbered, opening a smart fire on the main *kopje*. This was the signal for the Boer guns on the ridge to open, which they did with great precision on our two

THE OX TRANSPORT CROSSING THE MODDER RIVER

batteries, inflicting serious loss in a few minutes, and sending an occasional shell into the somewhat closely packed squadrons, though happily inflicting little loss there.

Meanwhile two Naval 12-pounders were struggling over some fearfully rough country to take a hand in the deal, but in doing so smashed the carriages of both guns; not to be denied, however, the gun crews man-handled their guns to the top of the intervening ridge, opening on the Boer guns with great effect, and the guns from the two horse-batteries joining in the fire on the same mark, the fire from the Boer guns were quickly reduced.

The advanced ridge thus held by the Boers was connected with their main position by a "*nek*," some 1000 yards long, sloping gradually to the plain we occupied, and quite practicable for horses as far as could be seen. No reconnaissance of the ground had, of course, been possible, but having got the guns under control, French perceived his opportunity, and gave the word to gallop through this break in the enemy's position, cut his forces in two, and if the gods favoured us, take his guns.

Then was seen a spectacle such as no man of this generation had ever witnessed, or will probably ever witness again— some 3000 cavalry charging a set position defended by guns and strongly held by concealed riflemen. Led by the 16th, who had been in advance, and who inclined sharply to their left, the 9th taking ground to their right, and forming the first line, then came the Second Brigade—the Households, 10th Hussars, and 12th Lancers, whilst Porter's Brigade—the Carabineers, Greys, and 6th Inniskillings, and Australians formed the third line, with the Rimington Guides and Mounted Infantry thrown in.

The onset was made at a hand-gallop, and the Boers, with their usual quickness of perception, didn't wait with their guns for the issue, but were off with them like a shot. It is the fashion to express admiration of the skill with which the Boers withdraw their guns, and perhaps, with a limited supply and no means of supplementing it, the policy may be a right one, but not by such uses are great triumphs won. One held one's breath,

THE CAVALRY DIVISION NEARING THE MODDER:
GENERAL FRENCH GIVING ORDERS.

expecting to see a whole squadron mowed down by shrapnel or case, but though the rattle of the Mauser was continuous, our men swept on. The dust rising under the horses' feet was punctuated with little spits kicked up by rifle bullets, and to the crackle of the Mauser was added the reverberating thunder of some 12,000 hoofs.

It was a stirring moment. A squadron would sweep by, its leader, with sparkling eyes, cheering forward his men with all the characteristic motions of a huntsman lifting his hounds. Presently the whole scene wrapped itself in a circling coil of dust, and though the hiss of rifle bullets seemed incessant, like the effect of the archbishop s curse, "nobody seemed one penny the worse."

But now as the connecting ridge was approached the firing, instead of redoubling itself, began to die out. Only on the left, whither the 16th had directed their charge, on the advanced ridge itself where the Boer guns had been, did it still continue; the three Boer guns had gone instantly as our lancers began to gallop, but a body of Boer riflemen, rushing to their horses, which had been hidden in a depression of the hills, found that a lucky shell from our guns had killed some forty outright; their riders therefore, reduced to the primitive means of locomotion known as Shanks' pony, continued to fight the ridge against the advancing lancers.

Lieutenant Hesketh, leading a half squadron, was shot, with two of his men, within thirty yards of the Boers, who, having then emptied their magazines, promptly put up a white flag, but our men were too close for this to avail. The Boer main position, though evacuated more promptly, was in such difficult ground that their forces had by no means cleared it when our squadrons swept over the *nek*, and our men galloped into the flying *burghers*, who jettisoned everything they could cast away in the effort to escape, carrying off, nevertheless, a few ugly wounds.

We ascertained subsequently that the Boer right wing, cut off in this fashion from the main body, retired precipitately on Cronje's camp at Magersfontein, spreading dismay and confu-

RUNNING THE 4.7 GUN INTO ACTION

sion among them, and exhibiting their lance thrusts and sabre cuts in proof of the desperate nature of the British attack, thus establishing the panic which broke up Cronje's Magersfontein *laager* that same night. There was no show of resistance for the rest of the day, but whenever we came to an eminence, far in the distance we could see a rapidly retreating little cloud of dust in almost every direction.

This little engagement, a mere affair of outposts as it seems, measured either by its duration, the amount of resistance, or the butcher's bill, was nevertheless the decisive battle of the war. It was the beginning of the *débâcle* which relieved our three beleaguered garrisons, and settled us in Bloemfontein.

After a long halt at a farm, with two excellent wells for watering, the advance on Kimberly was resumed, and about 3 p.m. we topped a ridge commanding a view of the distant town. The sight was a curious one; the town is rather an agglomeration of debris heaps and tall iron chimneys, as seen from the distance, with however a grateful show of real trees, not the Noah's Ark trees of the South African veldt.

The bombardment was still continuing with apparently unabated vigour, but as we sat in our saddles waiting for the final dispositions in which the Boer battle array was to be actually assailed, point after point of the Boer lines sank into silence. The next hour seemed of an endless tedium, and before it had sped we felt that even our clothes had taken fire in the burning heat, whilst we experienced the sensations of the cat on hot bricks if we dismounted to ease our mounts. Doubtless the impatience for a long delayed event is accountable in some degree for these sensations of a great discomfort.

Convinced that our immediate front was clear of the enemy, at a few minutes to four Lieutenant-Colonel Patterson, the veteran volunteer of Australia and the author, rode into the town. At the Beaconsfield barrier two lieutenants of the Town Guard dashed out of their trenches to welcome the first outsiders who had ridden into Kimberley for four months. From them we learned with what sinking hearts the gallant defenders had first caught sight of the relieving force. Without a notion that the Boer cordon had been broken, they viewed the cavalry division as it first came into sight as an overwhelming reinforcement to the enemy, beneath which their defences must be swept away.

Proceeding on into the town we met Colonel Kekewich, its gallant defender, coming out with his staff to receive General French, who, however, had become sharply engaged with the Boer rear covering the evacuation of their works at Fort Susannah.

The welcome of Kimberley to its relievers was equal to its unexpectedness. A stubborn defence under almost impossible conditions had been maintained. Despite some divisions of council caused by the *imperium in imperio* of a huge and all-powerful corporation like De Beers, and the masterful personality of Mr. Rhodes, the very utmost had been made of the town's resources; the ridiculously inadequate Imperial garrison had been strengthened by the resources of the great company and the gallant spirit of the inhabitants.

The artillery, which was perhaps powerful enough, if one of its projectiles hit a Boer, to occasion a severe headache, was reinforced by one really powerful gun, which was actually made in the town during the siege, and which for two days quite dominated the besieging guns, but was then in its turn wholly outranged by a gun delivering a shot of no lbs., with which the habitable part of the town was heavily bombarded, the Boers naively saying, "Oh no! we don't bombard the earthworks, we should not hurt anybody there, but by shelling the town we shall kill or wound so many people, the inhabitants will insist on a surrender." Curiously enough a shell from this big gun killed Mr. Labram, the builder of the English gun, "Long Cecil."

De Beers again came to the commandant's relief, by arranging to place, and actually placing, between three and four thousand women and children below ground in one of its mines, out of reach of shells, and to the De Beers had been due the overcoming of the water difficulty, when the Vaal River supply had been cut by the enemy. Well might the utmost resources of this most powerful company be made available, since to its existence alone was due the necessity for defending Kimberley.

CHAPTER 12

Cronje Beaten Back

Quick to recognise the moment for withdrawal, the Boer "Long Tom" had fired a round into the town late on Thursday afternoon, and had immediately been limbered up and retired towards Warrenton, a direction followed by about one-third of their forces, the remainder accompanying Cronje. To deal first with the smaller body retiring north, the garrison made an ineffectual attempt to retard the Boer guns on the evening of 15th, but the Boers, by leaving a strong rearguard with one 12½-inch at Dronfield, neutralised this move, and, more- over, offered a very stubborn resistance to French on the following day, when, moving out before daylight to the north-east, he swept round, encountering sharp resistance at Macfarlanes.

This he overcame after some loss, and enveloped the Dronfield *laager*, but the enemy clinging on desperately, he withheld an attack, considering the position untenable, which its occupation by a detachment of Cape Police and capture of the single gun at daylight next morning proved an accurate forecast. The Boers suffered heavily in defending this hill.

Meantime Cronje, whose camp had been filled with alarm on Thursday forenoon by the wounded fugitives from French's fight near Randheuvel Drift, had commenced his retreat the same night. The siege was raised, and there was no object in waiting to give battle on the old ground, whilst it was imperative to cover Bloemfontein as promptly as possible.

With very sound judgment, therefore, Cronje decided upon

a line of retreat in rear of French, and ahead of Tucker's division of infantry. Happily Tucker's scouts, finding this movement across his front during Thursday night, enabled him to throw his division on Cronje before he had slipped through, and an obstinate running fight was maintained all day. The Boers had neither the desire nor the heart to stand; indeed the reverse was the case; but although they were completely disheartened by the sudden turn of events, they still fought stubbornly every foot of ground, pushing on their convoy as rapidly as possible.

French, coming in from Dronfield about 5 p.m. on the 16th, received a message from headquarters detailing the position, and begging that he would intercept the Boers somewhere in the neighbourhood of Koodoosrand, distant about thirty miles south-east from Kimberley.

Moving out at midnight on February 16 with three regiments—the Household Cavalry, 10th Hussars, and 12th Lancers, and two batteries, and a squadron of Rimington's Guides—French, with exhausted horses inadequately supplied, began, on a few hours' notice, a movement which would have been a formidable one under the most favourable conditions. Directing that the Carabineers (6th Dragoons), escorting the company of mounted sappers, should follow in support four hours later, whilst the remainder of the division was to move as soon and as quickly after as possible, French with his staff pushed on two hours after the column had left, with the determination to thrust in between Cronje and Bloemfontein at all hazards, and, putting himself at its head immediately it was overtaken, he pushed forward very rapidly, heading direct for Koodoosrand Drift.

At a few minutes to 5 a.m. the advance patrol sent in word that the Boer army in strength was slowly crossing at Wolvenkraal Drift, whilst the river banks were held by it in considerable force from Paardeberg, about three miles westward of Wolvenkraal to Koodoosrand, three miles eastward.

The Boer attention was centred upon two points, the crossing the Modder River to the south bank, commanding the roads to Bloemfontein, and the rear, whence they expected a renewed attack at any moment from our pursuing infantry. French's advance from an unexpected direction had, therefore, been absolutely unobserved until he was about as far from a ridge of gentle hills commanding the river valley as was the main Boer camp.

Some shells were thrown at them when we descended into the plain, about 9 a.m., which they replied to, and then ensued a race for the ridge between the 10th Hussars and a strong body of Boers. Fortunately the Boer ponies were not very fresh, and they had to ascend the slope, else the exhausted horses of the 10th could never have landed their riders narrow winners, as they just managed to do, and the Boers sheered off to an accompaniment of carbine bullets, sustaining, however, very trifling loss.

French hurried up his guns, threw round his left (the 12th Lancers), and developed an attack with all the audacity of the commander of a legion instead of a mere cohort, completely deceiving the Boers, who, recognising that they were once more in face of the redoubtable cavalry leader, had no curiosity to ascertain the particulars of his command, but redoubled their efforts to cross the river, a difficult task unmolested, but now suddenly grown impossible.

The excessive mortality amongst the Boer horses in the previous day's battle had reduced many of the Boers to the mobility of infantry; their transport was hampered for the same reason, and to these causes are to be attributed their apparent inertia, which opposed no stout resistance to French's advance, and the resolution to defend the ground on which they stood, which set them (though we did not then know it) to convert the much honeycombed banks of the river into a veritable Plevna.

The 12th had by this time seized the drift, and crossed the river at Koodoosrand in the most gallant way, but were forced back to the north bank, to which they clung tenaciously. The interception being thus accomplished, and French's supports having come up, he moved his main strength to his left front, leaving the ridge of hills overlooking the Boer *laager* strongly held.

But what had become of the infantry division, of whom his

latest news only a few hours previously was that they were heavily engaged with Cronje? Here was Cronje sitting at his feet like an old boar, with bared tusks and rather bloody sides, but there was no sign of any infantry division, nor was there an echo in the clear air of any battle proceeding elsewhere to account for its absence.

Nevertheless, it hadn't been "eaten up." General Tucker had been detailed to make a detour to the south, and strike in again to the river by Osfontein; and Kelly-Kenny and Macdonald's Brigade were held back, no doubt, to give Tucker sufficient time to execute his movement; at any rate it was not till past eleven that the first gun was heard away to the westward, betokening that the infantry division had come up.

There can be no reasonable doubt that but for the interposition of French, Cronje would have made good his well-planned retirement on Bloemfontein, as but six miles to the eastward he would have received an accession of strength from De Wet, and would have been on ground already being hastily prepared by the Boers for resistance. As the infantry came into action the Boer forces slowly contracted on the main *laager*, fighting stubbornly; the ridge won by the 10th in the morning was occupied by the Welsh Fusiliers and the Duke of Cornwall's Light Infantry, the arch of the ridge being taken up by artillery, including the 4.7 guns and 12-pounders of the Naval Brigade, and being known thenceforth as Artillery Hill.

Cronje's position was now a hopeless one, surrounded by an army flushed with success and at least three times as numerous as his own, his men tired, dispirited, footsore—it takes very little walking to make a Boer footsore—his camp commanded by artillery from every direction, his own stores both of food and ammunition inadequate; yet the stubborn old warrior (for despite the obloquy which justly surrounds his name, he is a gallant soldier) determined to fight it out to the bitter end.

Looking at his position from outside, it is small wonder that Lord Kitchener, who had come up late on Friday and assumed the command of the infantry division, determined to carry the position by assault on Sunday morning, the enemy having been pushed back into it only the previous day.

There is little doubt that had the attack been delivered from one direction only it would have succeeded, gallantly as the Boers fought; but on so circumscribed an area, the enemy on a level, actually below the feet of the attacking force, in these days of long-range rifles, an assault from three sides at once carries with it the seeds of its own failure; so it happened that that fatal Sunday cost us more in casualties than any single engagement of the war, except Spion Kop; and when we hauled off in the afternoon we had won absolutely nothing, but were seriously crippled with wounds, mostly self-inflicted.

Lord Roberts himself arrived on the field during the afternoon, and immediately laid himself out for a conquest of pressure instead of assault. During the following days, therefore, Cronje's camp was assiduously bombarded during the day and closely guarded at night; his wagons had been set on fire by our howitzers on Sunday, and only during an armistice arranged for Tuesday, to pick up his dead, was the fire extinguished.

CHAPTER 13

De Wet Fails to Save Cronje

These operations, naturally, had been viewed with increasing alarm at Pretoria, and instead of ordering an immediate assault upon Ladysmith, men had been recalled from Joubert's command to defend Bloemfontein. The only real defence of Bloemfontein was to capture Ladysmith.

On the 21st, the commandos were so near that it became necessary to operate against De Wet, and recover Kitchener Hill, which, by some extraordinary oversight, had been abandoned, although it commanded the main drift over the Modder River; and the previous day the Boers had boldly surprised and captured a strong patrol of Roberts' Horse at Osfontein, itself so close to the scene of operations that it subsequently was made headquarters. Accordingly, French moved round part of his division—the brigade commands were for the time broken up by the exigencies of the situation—in the rear of Artillery Hill, crossed the river at Paardeberg, and with the 10th and 12th and Household Cavalry, and two R.H.A. batteries, cleared Kitchener's Hill, after a resistance entirely disproportionate to the value of the position and the number of Boers holding it.

The previous day the enemy had captured three carts containing various stores, and these they made a great effort to get away, having an exaggerated idea of their importance. They were pursued in the doubtful light of early morning, under the belief they were light guns, but only one was overtaken, and whilst the pursuers were halted to discover what was the nature of the capture, a large body of Boers suddenly swept round a *kopje*, apparently under the belief they had us on the hip, and could gallop over our men caught unawares.

They were ignorant, it appeared, that a battery had been accompanying the chase, which, quickly unlimbering, poured in, at a range of about 800 yards, such a deadly fire of case shot as speedily altered their intentions, inflicting a loss of about eighty killed and wounded, and leaving fifty prisoners in our hands.

A part of the commando forced back attempted to pass up the river valley in French's rear; Gordon with the 3rd Brigade was, however, covering French's left flank, and this body came under range of his guns, and though he failed in an effort to reach them by crossing the 16th Lancers in pursuit, they still suffered severely.

On 23rd, Boer reinforcements began to arrive from Natal, and a body of *Zarps*, about 200 strong, who had fought on that side with great distinction, attempted to seize two *kopjes* slightly isolated from our position, but were repulsed after a sharp encounter from that nearest our lines. Retiring from that attack, they proposed to occupy the more distant *kopje*, which had taken no part in the encounter, and which they assumed therefore we did not hold; a company of the Buffs was however stationed upon it, and had watched the course of the fight, and though aware of the approach of the discomfited *Zarps* made no sign, but allowed them to come on to point-blank range and then opened a deadly fire which completed their discomfiture; eighty-four men immediately threw down their arms, and as the remainder had all been either wounded or killed, the commando was entirely destroyed.

These two days' work put an absolute end to the efforts from outside to relieve Cronje, and though there was further unimportant fighting whilst the leaguer continued, it was entirely of our seeking.

On the night of the 25th, about 9 p.m., a most furious musketry fire broke out from Cronje's camp, and for half-an-hour there was a continuous roar, but if this was intended to cover an effort to break out, the intention was abandoned.

On Monday evening Lord Roberts directed the Canadians to sap down from the north as near as possible to the Boer trenches that covered that side of the Boer camp and ran parallel with the river, and there was an expectation that this would environ the Boer camp within about 500 yards. About midnight the Canadians moved down, and with a covering party advanced a few yards, before the main body set to work throwing up a trench, working undiscovered till between 3 and 4 a.m. on Tuesday, February 27, when suddenly a murderous fire was opened upon them.

The advance party, realising that cover must be had, and that it was no more deadly to run forward than to run back, made a dash for the Boer lines, and as they had actually got within 60 yards instead of 600, they were almost instantly tumbling headlong into the Boer trenches, where they established themselves and awaited events, such Boers as were unable to escape from these trenches either being killed or surrendering.

The Boers naturally connected this attack with the anniversary of Majuba Day, and made up their minds that with daylight would come a furious assault; and, since their defences were already in part carried, urged upon Cronje prompt surrender, to which after much hesitation he agreed. Of actual combatants there were 2507 Free Staters and 1141 Transvaalers, exclusive of the wounded, doctors, and commissaries. The total number surrendering was 4027.

There were very few horses indeed alive, no cattle at all, and 120 wagons uninjured, beside a number partially burnt or damaged. The four 12½-pounder Krupps were all without breech pieces, the one Maxim was disabled, but the pom-pom was sound except for the water-jacket, which was penetrated and rendered incapable of rapid firing. There were between six and seven thousand Mausers (a large quantity had also been destroyed in the burning wagons) and over a million rounds of ammunition.

It is impossible to overestimate the moral effect of this sur-

Paardeberg: Cronje's *Lager*

render. It was not only that a powerful force had been hemmed in and captured with all its supplies and stores, but the fighting general, the stubborn and invincible Cronje, had been overborne. Round him had centred the main romance to the Boer mind of the Great Rebellion; he had been the leader in raising resistance to the English; and though he had not borne a part in the great battles of the Natal frontier, he it was who had captured Potchefstroom.

True, that capture had some not very creditable features about it, but that was only an evidence to the Boer mind of their leader's "slimness," and so reflected additional glory upon him, for in this country of inversions it is better to be "slim" than honourable. Among the irreconcilables, therefore, Cronje was a greater name than Joubert, and the surrender of Cronje was a far greater blow than any other disaster that could have befallen the Boer arms.

PAARDEBERG: CRONJE'S *LAGER*

CHAPTER 15

Advance on Bloemfontein

The despatch of the 4000 prisoners having been promptly effected, the way seemed open for an immediate advance on the enemy's capital, and but for the shortness of fodder for horses and mules this might have instantly commenced, but the supply service had never recovered the loss of 210 wagons at Waterval a fortnight earlier.

In passing, one may justly comment upon the extraordinary inadequacy of an escort of one officer and forty-six men to guard so tempting a bait through a country known to be strongly held by the enemy, for French's advance had thrust back the Boer commando into the hills lying between Jacobsdal and the Riet River, whilst the advance of Macdonald's Brigade through Jacobsdal from Modder River Camp had prevented their retreat even had they desired it. All this was known, yet we despatch a convoy worth half a million of money and of inestimable value in the usefulness of its contents, under the enemy's very nose with a ridiculously insufficient guard.

Even then so excellent a defence did the escort (a half company of the Gordons) make, aided, as they most gallantly were, by all the wagon conductors, that they held the enemy at bay until reinforcements arrived, but unfortunately orders also came that if the convoy could not be extricated it was to be abandoned, and since all the oxen had been lost there seemed no alternative to abandonment, which was accordingly made.

The entire circumstances surrounding this transaction are of a kind which warrant the demand for the institution in the army of a system of penalties for blunders. In the sister service, if the captain of a ship gets his vessel aground he is probably dismissed the service; but with the army blunders of a far more culpable kind pass without any consequences to the blunderer, though the results may be terribly disastrous and of fatal consequence to others.

In this case the movements of a cavalry division were hampered by an easily preventable loss, hundreds of horses and mules succumbed to the combination of too much work with too little food, and not only were general movements delayed for supplies, but field operations were rendered slower and less effective.

Errors are the heritage of humanity, and no army, no matter how successful its campaign, but has suffered from a bad blunder at some part of it; but without doubt the fact that a blunderer goes unpunished, even unreprimanded, has a tendency to increase error.

Not till March 6 was it possible to move, and even then it was on a very slender supply of provender that the advance commenced. That day the cavalry division moved back in a southwesterly direction to Osfontein, and bivouacked at the farmhouse there.

At 2.30 a.m. the troops were again on the move. Striking away from the river towards Petrusburg, through which village Tucker's infantry division was to advance, whilst the cavalry were to turn off to the left as soon as they cleared the south end of the Koodoosrand Hills lying to the south of the river, in which the Boers had been entrenching themselves, Kelly-Kenny's division was to advance simultaneously straight up the river valley, having the main Boer position thus between itself and the cavalry, whilst the Guards and the Highland Brigades moved parallel along the north bank, driving the Boers out of their positions, and capturing one gun which had been rendered useless under the heavy shell-fire of the Naval Brigade.

About 6 a.m. the cavalry were saluted by two Boer guns from the western *kopjes* terminating the southern end of this range of hills. The Boer shells fell with great accuracy, and one was impressed with the ever new wonder of shells bursting amongst a group of horses and men and everybody escaping injury. We slowly drew out of fire, but for half-an-hour shells had been pitching well amongst us, yet there were no casualties.

Then as we turned again towards the left, now marching due east, and having the Boer positions due north, heavy rifle firing opened, followed again by shell-fire. Keeping out of range of rifle fire from the entrenchments the advance continued, when at 8.25 a.m. the Boers suddenly abandoned their advanced position and retired precipitately upon the river.

So far our operations had been admirably conducted, whilst those of the man—De Wet—who has since become notorious, were of the feeblest kind, for he had allowed a big turning movement to develop itself under his very nose without offering any practical resistance.

Shell-fire, however good, is practically as ineffective as the operations of a successful fleet without a land army to co-operate with it.

But from this moment the character of the operations was to change; ours were to be marked by utter feebleness, whilst De Wet was to display great skill and cleverness. French, for some reason unknown, was quite "off his game," whether it was due to over-anxiety to enmesh the Boer force, or whether he had positive instructions, is unknown, but he suddenly at this juncture contracted his enveloping movement, doubled his right in upon his centre where the ground emphasised this contraction by the closing in of the foothills, and we were all at once involved in a tiresome constriction.

The Boers, who up to this point had been rapidly pushed back, were now holding a ridge on our right front very stubbornly, and taking advantage of somebody's error in ordering a squadron of the 2nd Brigade to abandon a farm and garden which we had seized and which covered our right; none of our forces replacing this squadron, a party of Boers pluckily dashed into it and actually turned our right.

A HEAP OF BOER MAUSERS AFTER PAARDEBERG

French, whilst this was happening, had quickly perceived the situation, and extricating a gun of P Battery, which had got into difficulties under the rifle fire from this farm, which cost us some loss, amongst others the gallant David Keswick shot dead, and Bailey badly wounded, both with the reserve squadron of the 12th close under the farm, which they might just as easily have occupied when the 16th moved on, he quickly put matters to rights, and drove the Boers out of the farm, freeing the gun of P Battery; then moving rapidly forward on his interrupted line of advance, he made good use of an opportunity of shelling the Boers who were steadily retreating up the river valley. Then once more the demon of miscalculation took possession of him, and he repeated his blunder of the morning with precisely similar results.

De Wet had a heavy wagon convoy with him at Poplar Grove, and undoubtedly the stubborn defence he had developed was to save this and his guns. Incidentally, too, Mr. Kruger was that morning in his camp begging the *burghers* to stand firm; indeed one of his exhortations was interrupted by some of our shells, which fell uncomfortably near, when he belied the reputation of a life, and hurriedly drove off towards Bloemfontein, though even then he gave orders to his police escort to shoot the horses of any of his *burghers* who attempted to follow him by passing through the gate marking the boundary of the farms Poplar Grove and Waaihoek, an order that was actually begun to be carried out, until it was found that its effect might be very different to that intended by Kruger.

Had French continued due east he would have cut the Bloemfontein road a few miles ahead, because the river here bends towards his line of march, and though Kruger would probably have escaped, many of the wagons, and probably the guns, must have fallen into our hands.

Instead, by again doubling in on his centre, though he enfolded the major part of the Boer force, he cramped his own operations, failed to head off the Boer retreat, and allowed them to squeeze through. Had he continued his easterly course he would have cut the Boer line of retreat at a particularly difficult bit of road, and had it come off all their wheeled transport must have been taken; the Boers, therefore, offered a splendid resistance.

Perceiving this, French instantly took steps to extend his right, and as it was favourable country he would even then have accomplished his purpose but for one of the most gallant acts performed by the Boers during the war.

A low ridge screened French's force from a long plain sloping back to the river, and the General had just given orders for this to be seized, and was in the act of riding up to it with his staff, when the heads of a small number of Boers appeared over the crest. Rapidly dismounting, they drove French himself straight back with a withering fire, and inflicted a good many casualties.

A charge would instantly have given us the ridge, but horses had already been twelve hours under the saddle, and could not raise a gallop.

Had P Battery been promptly turned on the ridge with shrapnel all would have gone well; but a gunner, contemptuously observing that such a small body was no mark for a battery, continued to direct its fire against the Boer guns. French sent word to open on the ridge with shrapnel; but either the message was misunderstood, or before it reached the battery the officer in command found his men going down under rifle fire; at any rate, instead of changing direction of fire, he began limbering up, when French rode up himself and somewhat forcibly directed what was necessary, and after a few rounds the ridge was cleared.

As far as we could discover these Boers suffered no loss; our estimate of their number was forty, and we found subsequently they actually numbered thirty-seven. They had inflicted about that number of casualties upon us, had tied up an entire cavalry brigade for an hour, and had enabled every- thing to be got away. Truly a gallant deed, of which any army might be proud.

There was now nothing to be done but to get back to the

river and bivouac for the night.

Never was cold water more welcome, or a swim more delightful.

The result of the day's operations may, however, be justly summed up as an exceeding great triumph for French, despite the errors described, for De Wet had been for at least ten days preparing the position from which he was ready to defy the whole British army.

He had, in fact, abandoned it on the mere approach of the cavalry division; he had not only abandoned it, but had only narrowly escaped from it with his guns and his transport wagons, and these last got off at the expense of a considerable portion of their loads, and only by the devoted bravery of a small part of his force.

If our cavalry general had not been free of error in his conduct of the day's operations, he is at least entitled to count the general result of the day as a triumphant example of his great theory of taking a strongly-fortified position with a numerically inferior force by marching round it.

There was enough fodder jettisoned from the flying wagons to find the greater part of the animals a feed of corn; whether the rearmost brigades were as lucky is another question.

BOER TRENCHES AT POPLAR GROVE. THE TRENCHES ARE ONLY
HALF-FINISHED AND THE TOOLS LEFT BEHIND.

Chapter 15

French Deals Heavy Blows

Next morning there was the usual difficulty of supply before a start could be made; there was some desultory firing between outposts; but the enemy was in full flight, intending to offer resistance at Abram's Kraal, and to make a desperate stand at Baine s Vley, whither a large portion of Joubert's Natal force was on its way.

Our move for the day was only six or seven miles along the river, and as supplies had come up we advanced next morning, March 10, on Abram's Kraal, situated among a range of wooded *kopje*s about three miles south of the river on which the range abuts.

Here on very favourable ground we found De Wet in force, posted with three guns, his right resting on the river, and his left pushed out in some scattered *kopje*s, to which he obstinately clung.

The action commenced at 10 a.m. Porter's Brigade being in advance, the 2nd Cavalry Brigade was acting with Tucker's division, which was advancing on Kelly-Kenny's right? converging on Bloemfontein through Petrusberg. A prolonged fight ensued, in which our guns gradually overpowered the Boer artillery by number and sheer hard fighting, though quite over-ranged. Pushing steadily through with his right, Porter had enfiladed the Boer position, and when the infantry came up he had been able to report a ridge in its immediate front clear of the enemy, who was in full retreat.

Either the retirement had been a feint, or else the enemy was able to re-occupy this ridge unobserved, but certainly a part of the Boer force had been exposed in retiring from it to our shell-fire, suffering heavy loss.

Over forty dead Boers were subsequently found on this spot. General Porter had two batteries at this point, and T Battery was so placed as to command the *nek* which the retreating Boers crossed, whilst U Battery was moving to find fresh ground.

The general, for the moment without a galloper, asked the writer to carry a message to Major Taylor of U Battery to move to the front of the hill on which T Battery was placed to enfilade more completely the Boer position, pointing out the designed spot; delivering the message with exactitude the writer was quite close to the battery when it opened fire, but under complete cover, and thus able to witness one of the most extraordinary contests of the war.

The guns had moved on to open ground to command a *nek* between the ridge evacuated and a covering ridge in its rear, about 2300 yards distant from the battery. As the limber horses were retiring the Boers opened from this second ridge with rifle and pom-pom fire, and poured in such a hail of lead that it seemed nothing could survive; the horses were quickly under cover, and the fire being directed on the battery did not suffer much. Then began a rain of lead, which looked as though it must destroy every living thing round the guns; the firing from the pom-pom seemed continuous, and the rattle of the Mausers not less so.

The battery so far had not fired a shot, and every man was down flat on his face. Standing within two hundred yards I wondered whether every man of them was not shot dead; then one of the guns answered with a shell beautifully pitched, and the gunners dropped flat again; then another gun, and in a few minutes they were all at it, searching the whole length of the ridge; and a few minutes later, accompanying Major Hathaway, French's staff surgeon, I went down to the battery to find only seven casualties (one fatal), and all but two of these due to rifle bullets and not to the shells.

Captain Rouse's cheerful greeting, "that was a hot corner; I don't mind their shells, but confound their rifles," gave a new cue to one's thoughts. The cavalry had already gone on, in pursuance of its plan of turning the Boer left, and gained the main road as it emerged from these hills, leaving the infantry, as we believed, merely to occupy the ground we had won.

Never was there a more mistaken idea. Whether the whole movement of the Boers had been a ruse or not cannot be stated; but anyhow, as Kelly-Kenny's division came up it had a most obstinate fight to win these very ridges we had seen evacuated. The Boer guns did not come into action; but, despite that, the Boer riflemen showed desperate fight, and were finally dislodged at the charge.

The Essex Regiment covered itself with distinction, rushing the ridge with fixed bayonets, though suffering heavily, losing two officers who could ill be spared in Captains Eustace and Parsons, to the latter of whom the rare honour of a posthumous Victoria Cross was accorded.

Our casualties, which fell very largely upon the infantry, amounted for the day to 424 in all. But the Boer loss was heavier than either side had (so far as was known) suffered up to that date. We buried 170 Boers on the two ridges, and 42 were later found and buried on the *nek* where our guns had caught them in the retirement. Our loss in actual killed at Magersfontein amounted to 171, at Colenso to 135.

Our failure to capture the Boer big gun was due to the utter exhaustion of the cavalry horses. Our turning movement completely succeeded, and we came round on to the main road in sight of the retiring guns; the 12th Lancers, indeed, got within half a mile of the rearmost gun, but it was the last effort of the horses, many of whom had to be dismounted and led back to the bivouac. The Boers again showed great courage, stopping their retreat, and sniping the regiment back to the camp in the gathering darkness.

The result of this action was much more conclusive than the

mere story of the fight conveys. Once more the cavalry had enveloped a Boer position, and forced its evacuation after a comparatively slight resistance, and only the proximity of the infantry had forced a fierce rearguard action, in which, whilst sustaining loss, we had demonstrated the impossibility of resisting a determined advance, and had inflicted upon an enemy holding entrenched positions loss infinitely greater than that suffered by the assaulting troops. The fugitives, who entered the Free State capital between Saturday night and Sunday night, carried a story of the utter hopelessness of the struggle, and the invincibility of the English attack.

The Boer retreat on Baine's Vley was continued through the night, and the next day there was no vestige of an enemy in the whole country-side. Our bivouacs for the night were at Doornkop and Aasvogels Kop, twenty-four miles from Bloemfontein, and near a most beautiful and extensive artificial lake or dam, many hundreds of acres in extent—a rare boon to the hard-marched men. All the farmhouses had been hastily vacated by their owners, but though empty all were bearing at least one white flag; some, one at each corner. But rarely did one enter a house but one found some rifle cartridges, and this though no systematic search was made.

It might well then have been notified to the inhabitants that to exhibit the white flag on an unoccupied house would entail some punishment to the owners on the pacification of the country, and if exhibited on a house in which ball cartridges or arms were found, the house would be instantly destroyed.

CHAPTER 16

Capture of Bloemfontein

The advance on Monday was entirely uneventful till near
nightfall. Leaving Doornkop we struck the valley of the Kaal
Spruit, encountering no resistance, and finding the scattered
farms almost entirely unoccupied; towards midday we approached a farm of more pretension than most, which proved to
be vacant, and to belong to a man of some note in recent South
African history—Judge Gregorowski.

It was at present in the occupation of one Daniel Louw, and
was protected by a notice written in English in a round school-
boy hand, pinned to an organ in the front room, warning that
any non-respecter of the Lares and Penates would be made to
suffer for his desecration in the future life. The provost-marshal
proved, however, a more efficient protector. The column was
halted here for two hours, which seemed tedious to some of us
in the tension of an impending trial by battle.

However we were again afoot in due time, and the advance
was now directed to cut the railway about the locality of Leu-
wkop, some ten miles to the south of Bloemfontein.

The main road from Edenburg to Bloemfontein runs here on
the western side of the railway, and parallel to it, and as we approached a trap was observed driving rapidly towards the capital,
which, on being intercepted, was found to contain a Mr. Palmer,
an English resident of the Free State, who was also a member of
the Executive Council, and was hastening into Bloemfontein, in
response to an urgent summons to a council meeting. Having

114

explained his position and intentions to General French, and having asked to be excused from answering any questions bearing upon the intentions or preparedness of the Free Staters, he was entrusted with the commander-in-chief's summons to surrender, and permitted to proceed on giving an undertaking to deliver the message that night to the president, or failing him to the authorities of the town. It was evident there was a full intention to offer a strong resistance, and General French sent forward a squadron of the 6th Inniskillings to reinforce the Greys, who were doing the advance patrol.

Approaching a farm on our right front, we surprised the owner in the act of leaving by cart and four horses; being arrested, he gave the name of John Steyn, a brother of the president, and his family were found still in possession of their home, and so remained. Steyn was placed on parole, and now expressed very different sentiments to those he had voiced about a year earlier when in a public speech he had advocated the cause of Mr. Kruger, and commended his withdrawal from the Bloemfontein Conference.

Meanwhile another English farmer had ridden in from the hills on our left front, and informed Major Lawrence that the Boers were in strength holding the hills stretching in a semicircle from Baine's Vley to a point about a mile beyond the railway, which passed through a narrow gap due north from Steyn's farm; that they were entrenched in the hills above his farm, and had several guns emplaced.

French, although the day was far spent, was bent on seizing the range of covering hills, and pushed forward his right across the railway. To the left of the railway a pleasant valley pushed far up into the hills, and sheltering it two isolated wooded *kopjes*, of no great height, stood out in the plain; towards these French directed the Inniskilling Dragoons, whose patrols pushed into them to find them unoccupied, but immediately they showed beyond them a furious rifle fire broke out.

These *kopjes* were now clearly of immense importance; their possession enabled us to approach within striking distance of the

Boer position, yet no move was made to occupy them in force, until French sent a peremptory message that it should be done. Fortunately the Boers made no attempt to regain them, for which they had ample time, and could easily have overpowered the half-dozen carbines which were holding them. The Carabineers (6th Dragoons) had also seized an outlying *kopje* still more to the left, and directly fronting the Boer position.

The Greys were now under a furious fire, and the Boer guns were opening upon them. French's impatience and his realisation, doubtless, of the desperate value even of moments, led him forward under a sharp fire to press his advance upon the hills to the east of the railway. The Greys, suffering under a tremendously heavy fire from the hills on their right flank, were struggling to accomplish this, the weakness of the fire from these hills east of the line indicating them as the point to attack.

Meantime orders to hurry forward supports, especially the guns, had been repeatedly sent back, though moments were too precious to delay the attack for want of them, and the exhausted condition of the horses rendering speedy reinforcement impossible.

The railway is fenced on either side by stout fencing of considerable height and much heavier wire than ordinary, and this offered a tremendous barrier to the Greys, as well as the Mounted Infantry and Rimingtons coming up in support; cutting the wires was a most difficult job in any case, not diminished by the continuous fire from the Boers. However, a gap was cut, and U Battery, R.H.A., coming into action, opened hotly on the Boer guns and riflemen, quickly reducing their fire.

The Greys were thus enabled to seize a line of *kopjes* which almost commanded the town; there was only one other row in front of them; and in the deepening dusk French examined them, and directed that they were to be seized later, when it was quite dark, as they seemed to be evacuated; whilst the Greys swept over the hill commanding the railway from the east, with the Mounted Infantry in support, and though the falling darkness did not diminish the Boer artillery fire, which continued long after darkness fell, yet that only served to confirm our knowledge that this brilliant piece of work had placed Bloemfontein in our hands.

The task of seizing the most advanced line of *kopjes* fell to Major Scobell and twelve men of the Greys, who made a dash for the most important one before daybreak, and arrived there just as a party of Boers were on the way back to reoccupy it. Several of them were hit, the remainder driven off, and the hill safely held.

But even this was not the measure of French's success, for, realising that to instantly sever the railway communication with the north would be not only to throw all stores in the Free State capital into our hands, but to cut off all chance of effective assistance reaching it, Major Hunter Weston had been despatched about midnight with a small escort to accomplish this purpose.

Right gallantly did he fulfil the task. With an escort of eight Mounted Infantry he left French's headquarters; pushing round eastwards he struck the railway about seven miles beyond the capital, and, having wrenched out some rails, proceeded along the line to find a culvert. There were numerous parties of Boers moving, or on picket duty, all of whom had to be avoided; but the culvert, when found, proved to be guarded.

Nevertheless, by creeping forward, a charge of dynamite was successfully laid and exploded, and the line was cut effectively. Major Weston and his men succeeded in rejoining the escort, and getting off with no loss, despite having, as dawn broke, to charge through a Boer patrol which had stumbled accidentally across their path, and only one slight wound amongst the party resulted.

This was a most invaluable piece of work; not only did it prevent reinforcements from Pretoria (and 3000 men were on the way, under Joubert, and indeed were notified for arrival that afternoon), but even more important was the means of the prevention of the escape of thirty locomotives, over a hundred trucks, a number of carriages, and about a thousand tons of coal, loaded in readiness for withdrawal.

This action, which has largely escaped notice, chiefly by reason of its most complete success, is as brilliant as anything that has occurred in the war. French seized, with under 1000 men and one battery, the key to a range of fortified hills, held by 6000 men, according to the information in his possession when the attack was made, with troops that had marched eighteen or twenty miles during the day, and with darkness already falling.

By his prompt action the capture of the town became inevitable, and by it he was enabled to cut the railway, force the Boer retirement through a difficult country, prevent reinforcements reaching them, and gain for himself transport facilities which achieved the replenishment of stores a full month earlier than could in any other case have been possible.

The following morning, March 13, after a pretence at resistance, the Boer leaders withdrew their guns, and a deputation came out at ten, and surrendered the town of Bloemfontein.

With the capture of the Free State capital, the second stage of the war ended. The conditions of the contest had been entirely reversed, almost unvarying Boer successes had characterised the first stage. British territory was in every direction invaded, and British garrisons were being beleaguered; the second stage, the duration of which was only one month and a day, relieved two of the three garrisons, placed the Free State capital in our hands, and gave us the redoubtable Cronje with his 4000 men as prisoners.

www.ingramcontent.com/pod-product-compliance
Lightning Source LLC
Chambersburg PA
CBHW031901090426
42741CB00005B/598